Advance Praise

"*The Power of Cute* examines an acute yet virtually unnoticed part of contemporary society, the rise of cuteness. A joy to read, this book is terrifyingly brilliant and continuously surprising, filled with subtle insights and wonderful theorizing."
—Jeffrey C. Alexander, Yale University

"From powerlessness to tyranny, and from the fluffy dog in the window to Kim Jong-il's hairstyle, 'the cute' raises the abysmal issue of the world's desire for meaninglessness. Comforting and uncanny at the same time, cuteness incarnates nihilism as plenitude, infantilism as art, and desexualization as seduction. Simon May's humorous and profound book explores the secret dimensions of a new religion, raising the question: Is cuteness an attribute of God?"
—Catherine Malabou, Kingston University London

"We think we have power over cute things—but maybe the boot is on the other foot, and cute things manipulate us. *The Power of Cute* considers the notion that when we find things or people cute, ambivalence is in the air: on the one hand, cute things are infantile and unthreatening, on the other hand, uncanny or unsettling. This intelligent and thought-provoking book breaks new ground."
—Simon Blackburn, author of *Mirror, Mirror*

"In this highly readable and erudite book, Simon May develops a theory of 'the cute.' May probes a range of cases, particularly of artificial cuteness—Hello Kitty, Pokémon, E.T., Kewpie dolls—and gives searching reflections on what the ascendancy of cute might reflect about our broader societal values and present historical moment."
—Andrew Huddleston, Birkbeck, University of London

The Power of Cute

ʻute

Simon May

PRINCETON UNIVERSITY PRESS

Princeton and Oxford

Copyright © 2019 by Simon May

Published by Princeton University Press
41 William Street, Princeton, New Jersey 08540
6 Oxford Street, Woodstock, Oxfordshire OX20 1TR

press.princeton.edu

All Rights Reserved
Library of Congress Control Number: 2018957590
ISBN 978-0-691-18181-3

British Library Cataloging-in-Publication Data is available

Editorial: Sarah Caro, Hannah Paul, Charlie Allen
Production Editorial: Terri O'Prey
Text Design: Pamela Schnitter
Jacket/Cover Design: Amanda Weiss
Jacket/Cover Credit: *Maneki-neko* (Japanese "welcoming cat")
courtesy of Italika / iStock
Production: Jacqueline Poirier
Publicity: Caroline Priday and Julia Haav
Copyeditor: Molan Goldstein

This book has been composed in Cormorant Garamond
and Gotham

Printed on acid-free paper ∞

Printed in the United States of America

10 9 8 7 6 5 4 3 2 1

To Mimi, guru of Cute

Contents

Illustrations

Preface

My aim in this short book is to investigate a sensibility and a style that are everywhere around us and yet on which philosophy has had next to nothing to say. It is not to ask whether Cute is or isn't in good taste, or even what good and bad Cute might be.[1] (I find myself both strongly attracted to some of its manifestations and strongly repelled by others.) Rather, my guiding questions are these: Whether we love it or excoriate it, whether we think it trivial or compelling, perverse or harmless, what is the craze for Cute about? And why has it become so extraordinarily pervasive since the Second World War, especially in the United States and Japan?

I argue that Cute should be understood far more broadly than is generally the case.

Instead of being just about sweet, cuddly, vulnerable qualities that we see in people and things, it is, above all, about what happens when the Sweet (what is soft, harmless, innocent, artlessly charming, unencumbered by complexity, and usually small) gets uncanny, indeterminate—such as between child and adult, masculine and feminine, nonhuman and human, familiar and unfamiliar, powerless and powerful, unknowing and knowing—and even monstrous. But, crucially, in a lighthearted and often frivolous register.

To the extent that I am attempting to explore a term in common use, the meaning of which might seem obvious but in fact turns out to be richer and more elusive than we think, my approach is inspired by Susan Sontag's *Notes on "Camp"* and Harry Frankfurt's essay *On Bullshit*. It belongs to such an attempt at definition to mark off the phenomenon one is studying from neighboring ones. So I will ask how, for example, Cute relates to Sweet and Kitsch, just as Frankfurt asks how Bullshit differs from lying and bluffing, and Sontag, if she had written her essay a decade or two later, might have inquired how Camp is distinguished from Cool and Zany.

But my interest is not just to define Cute, to understand what makes us see things and people as cute, and to characterize the experience of Cute. Beyond that it is to ask: What light can the attempt to tease out the sensibility, the style, the mood, the way of being that Cute expresses shed on the era and the cultures in which it is so prevalent? In other words, what is it about our age that so favors the rise of Cute? And how can we use Cute to probe the zeitgeist?

The French spirit, Montesquieu suggested, possesses the art of speaking seriously about frivolous things and frivolously about serious things.[2] I hope I have been sufficiently "French" here to succeed in at least one of these respects.

The Power of Cute

1

Cute as a Weapon of Mass Seduction

Cute is colonizing our world. But why? And why, so explosively, in our times?

We might think Cute so trite as not to merit attention, and certainly not to be a worthy subject of investigation. Or so perverse, in the clichéd helplessness it foists on its objects, and perhaps relishes in them, as to deserve little more than scorn. So that it would be pointless at best to try to dig into something as superficial as the feline girl-figure Hello Kitty; Pikachu, the Pokémon monster; E.T., with its gangly shrunkenness; the ugly Cabbage Patch Kids; and the strange evolution of Mickey Mouse after the Second World War. Or perhaps we have become so accustomed to Cute that we don't notice its ubiquity—for example, in the proliferation of emojis, embraced by people of almost all ages and backgrounds; or in the abundance of cute-sounding brand names such as "Google" (and, for that matter, "Apple," whose logo teasingly links the personal freedom afforded by its devices to a primal symbol of rebellion: biting into the forbidden fruit in the Garden of Eden). All of which might be why so little has been written on the phenomenon and meaning of Cute and the relentless succession of faddish objects that give voice to it. We are strangely uncurious about it.

But what if Cute speaks of some of the most powerful needs and sensibilities of our contemporary world? What if, to adapt a phrase of Nietzsche, it is indeed superficial—but out of profundity?[1] What if Cute isn't just about powerlessness and innocence but also plays with, mocks, ironizes the value we attach to power—as well as our assumptions about who has power and who doesn't? What if it mesmerizes precisely because it isn't (or isn't seen as) only harmless, innocent, and cuddly, and therefore comforting in an impersonal world full of danger, but can also—as we find with the intentional distortion and ugliness of so many cute objects—express something richer, and truer to life: something that at the same time is experienced as unclear, unsafe, uncanny, defective, knowing—albeit in a playful register? What if this faintly menacing subversion of boundaries, this all-too-human indeterminacy—between the clear and the obscure, the wholesome and the irregular, the innocent and the knowing—when presented in Cute's lighthearted, teasing idiom, is central to its immense popularity?

What if, moreover, the explosion of Cute reflects one of the great developments of our age, at least in the West: the cult of the child? For the child is, I suggest, the new supreme object of love, which is, very gradually, replacing romantic love as the archetypal love, the must-have love, the kind of love without which no human life is deemed to be fully lived or maximally flourishing. And childhood is the new locus of the sacred—and so the place where, as a society and as an age, we most readily find desecration.

As we will see, there has been a remarkable coincidence between the rise of Cute since the mid-nineteenth century and the increasing valuation of childhood over almost exactly this same period—with both trends accelerating in tandem after the Second World War. Which, I will argue, in no way means that the craze for Cute is driven merely, or even primarily, by an urge to regress to childhood, to an imagined world of safety and simplicity; or that its motivation and aim are necessarily infantile.

Indeed, we must ask whether Cute doesn't also speak of a loss of faith in sharp distinctions between childhood and adulthood. For isn't childhood experience increasingly seen as determining everything important about adult life, as at work in all its key emotions and choices and doings? And, conversely, isn't the contemporary adult world—in particular, its intense concern with self-expression, authenticity, and sexuality—increasingly taken to pervade the child's?

❖

Cute objects, I am therefore proposing, aren't just infantile distractions from the anxieties of today's world, where breakneck competition and change are displacing people from their jobs, communities, and identities overnight. They aren't just sources of safe and reliable intimacy in an era that seems to be racing towards an explosion of fears, furies, grievances, and historic injustices, too many and too great to address or redress all at once. They aren't just avatars of soulless commercialism, or ways of escaping into a self-indulgent, empty, uncommitted existence. They aren't just ways of personalizing the artifacts of an impersonal world. Nor are they necessarily screens onto which stereotypes of innocence—especially of young feminine innocence—are projected. Though Cute can be, and, as we will see, has been widely accused of being, all these things, and though like most sensibilities—including most virtues, appetites, aesthetics, goods, and gods—it can be misused for unacceptable ends and its motives can become pervaded by cynicism, self-gratification, power-seeking, and violence, none of these features are intrinsic to it.

Instead Cute, I will suggest, is above all a teasing expression of the unclarity, the uncertainty, the uncanniness, the continuous flux or "becoming" that our era detects at the heart of all existence, living and nonliving. It is palpably ephemeral in the ever-changing styles and objects that exemplify it, which are nothing if not transient and lack any claim to lasting significance. It exploits the reality that when indeterminacy is pressed beyond certain points it becomes menacing: a reality that Cute is able to render beguiling precisely because it does so trivially, charmingly, unmenacingly—indeed, in a self-consciously laid-back style. It expresses an intuition that life has no firm foundations, no enduring, stable "being"; that, as Heidegger intimated, the only ground for living lies in the acceptance of its nongroundedness.[2] And it often does so with something like the "artifice and exaggeration,"[3] expressed in a manner that "dethrones the serious,"[4] or that fails in its seriousness, which Susan Sontag attributes to Camp.

This "unpindownability," as we might call it, that pervades Cute—the erosion of borders between what used to be seen as distinct or discontinuous realms, such as childhood and adulthood—is also reflected in the blurred gender of the many cute objects that appear hermaphroditic or indeterminate. (What gender is E.T., or Jeff Koons's *Balloon Dog*?) It is reflected, too, in their frequent blending of human and nonhuman forms. And indeed in their often undefinable age. For though cute objects might appear childlike, it can be strikingly hard to say, as with E.T., whether they are young or old—sometimes seeming to be, in human terms, both young and old. (E.T.'s wrinkled skin is "simultaneously that of a newborn and an elderly person."[5])

In such ways, Cute is attuned to an era that is no longer as wedded as it once was to hallowed dichotomies like masculine and feminine, sexual and nonsexual, adult and child, being and becoming, transient and eternal, body and soul, absolute and contingent, and even good and bad—dichotomies that once structured great ideals but that are now taken to be less hard-and-fast, more porous than had been traditionally assumed.

Moreover, Cute's celebration of indeterminacy is reflected, too, in its incompatibility, as a sensibility, with the modern cult of sincerity and authenticity, which has its origins in the eighteenth century and which assumes that each of us has an individual self—or at least a set of beliefs, feelings, drives and tastes—that uniquely identifies us and that we can both clearly grasp and know to be truthfully expressed. As we will see, the spirit of

Cute steps entirely aside from our prevailing faith that we can know—and control—when we are being sincere and authentic, let alone that others can know when we are being sincere and authentic.

And, although Cute can become hijacked by a desire for power, it also articulates, perhaps more fundamentally, a nascent will to repudiate the ordering of human relations by power, or at least to question our assumptions about who has power and to what end. This is a will that Cute can vividly convey precisely because it usually involves a relationship to a vulnerable object or to an object that flaunts, or flirts with, vulnerability. It is a will to liberation from the power paradigm that many, especially in the West and Japan, but perhaps ordinary Chinese people too, might be expected to affirm as an antidote to a century and more of unparalleled brutality.

In short: What if Cute isn't a frivolous distraction from the zeitgeist but rather a powerful expression of the zeitgeist?

❖

We are clearly talking of an ever-growing phenomenon that has already colonized large tracts of the globe and of our contemporary imagination. The axis of Cute has capitals in California and greater Tokyo, a rapidly increasing presence in China (very much including Hong Kong)—which might one day take over from Japan and the United States as the global engine of Cute—and outposts dotted about the rest of East Asia, for example, in Thailand, Singapore, and Taiwan, as well as in various European countries. Advertisements, consumer products, corporate names and logos—not to mention contemporary art—exploit its edgy charm, its self-conscious innocence, its spooky play on playfulness, its ironizing of itself, its seeming refusal of both hard reality and great ideals. Countless products, from computers to phones, from guns to food, from children's toys to calendars, from stockings to airplanes, from condoms to contact lenses, can be, and have been, branded with a cute logo. Even Lady Gaga saw fit to do a photo shoot in garish Hello Kitty garb.

Jeff Koons's famous "balloon dogs" perfectly exemplify the spirit of Cute, and show how it can be darker, more uncertain, and more ambiguous than mere sweetness.[6] *Balloon Dog (Red)* seems both powerful (made of stainless steel) and powerless (it lacks a face, a mouth, and eyes; its "balloons" are hollow). Its "innocence" is melancholic; its innocuousness arresting; its vulnerable demeanor offset by its huge size. (See fig. 1.1.)

Global hits like Bambi, Pokémon, E.T., Hello Kitty, and So Shy Sherri; artists like Takashi Murakami, Yoshitomo Nara, Jeff Koons, Mark Ryden, and Brecht Evens; cute modes of self-presentation such as emojis—all speak to our age with peculiar force, and not just to young people but to legions of adult fans, male and female, such as engineers, politicians, investment managers, doctors, and media celebrities. The core consumers of Hello Kitty are women aged eighteen to

FIG. 1.1 Jeff Koons, *Balloon Dog (Red)* (1994–2000). © Jeff Koons. Photo: AFP/Getty.

forty, running the gamut from performance artists to punk rockers, Wall Street bankers to porn stars;[7] and the cat-girl features in top-end fashion collections from New York to Milan and Tokyo. Adorable babies, puppies, and polar bears are cooed over by millions of grown men and women on innumerable websites devoted to all things cute. In Washington, DC, a panda cub born in the Smithsonian's National Zoo becomes an instant celebrity. All thirteen thousand tickets to see him are snapped up within a couple of hours, with many more fans waiting their turn in freezing temperatures. Soon afterwards, a movie about the severely cute emperor penguin is one of the greatest box-office hits ever for a documentary.[8] Over in Berlin, a polar bear cub dubbed "Cute Knut" attracts a global following of tens or hundreds of millions overnight, while back in early 2011, Heidi, a cross-eyed opossum whose large black-and-white eyes squint demurely towards her pointed pink snout, is front-page news in Germany's mass media, commanding almost as much attention as the world-historical "Arab Spring" then unfolding in Tunisia and Egypt.

❖

Yet such reflection on Cute as exists tends to miss the point by seeing its essence as helpless and easily exploitable vulnerability. And much of this reflection, especially in the West and Japan, though far less so in other parts of Asia, goes on to lament its infantilizing of the viewer (or else its expressing a will to be infantilized: to regress to a perhaps mythical childlike existence of unchallenging simplicity and pampered safety), its power to arouse a sleazy blend of pity and pleasure, its sly invitation to both caregiving and sadism, its sexualized aesthetic, as well as its subordination to—and fostering of—rampant consumerism.

This is certainly the dominant understanding of Cute. Thus Sianne Ngai, in a landmark essay, sees it as an "aestheticization of powerlessness," an "affective response to weakness," that revolves "around the desire for an ever more intimate, ever more sensuous relation to objects already regarded as familiar and unthreatening." Such affective responses to weakness can easily become brutal or deforming, one reason why Ngai, like others, says that violence is "always implicit in our relation to the cute object."[9]

Christine Yano, in her book tracking Hello Kitty's trek across the Pacific from Japan to the United States, characterizes Cute as "innocent, playful, guileless, appealing, and ultimately marketable"[10] and cites others who decry its "fake mall-bought conformity."[11] Gary Cross sees it as "wondrous innocence."[12] Natalie Angier, reporting the views of Denis Dutton, a philosopher of art, laments that the "rapidity and promiscuity of the cute response makes the impulse suspect, readily overridden by the angry sense that one is being exploited or deceived."[13] Sharon Kinsella, writing on "Cuties in Japan," sees the pervasiveness of *kawaii* (roughly the Japanese equivalent of cute) as reflecting "fashion-able infantilism."[14] Daniel Harris, in a widely quoted essay, lambastes it as an "antiquated religion of infantilism" that has governed parents' attitudes towards their offspring: a "portable utopia" of innocence and guile-lessness and other fetishized states that "we would *like* to see in children," who are forced "not only to be cute [in themselves] but to recognize and enjoy cuteness in others, to play the dual roles of actor and audience." "Because it aestheticizes unhappiness, help-lessness, and deformity," Harris also remarks, "it almost always involves an act of sadism on the part of its creator, who makes an uncon-scious attempt to maim, hobble, and embar-rass the thing he seeks to idolize."[15]

Indeed, Harris continues, "the cute world-view is one of massive human chauvinism," which forces human qualities onto non-human things. So that children's books, for example, impose on "dogs, cats, bears and pigs . . . the clothing and demeanor of human beings." The "narcissism of cuteness" means that "the cute vision of the natural world is a world without nature, one that annihilates 'otherness,' ruthlessly suppresses the non-human, and allows nothing, including our own children, to be separate and distinct from us." Cuteness, Harris maintains, "is ultimately dehumanizing, paralyzing its victims into comatose or semi-conscious things."[16]

That is quite a charge sheet. Aside from the almost unchallenged article of faith that human relations, including here between a child and a toy bear, are to be understood, first and foremost, as relations of power (a legacy of a very particular philosophical tradition fostered in modern times by figures such as Nietzsche and Foucault, which is itself overripe for questioning), surely even the harshest critic of Cute could see some merit in it insofar as it cultivates the nurturing and self-giving instincts?

Indeed, there is a school of thought, following the pioneering work of Konrad Lorenz, which we will consider in chapter 2, that regards cuteness as a prime trigger of precisely those instincts. Thus, the cultural theorist Joshua Paul Dale argues that "cuteness is fundamentally an appeal to others: an invitation to sociality," in responding to which "one discovers oneself *already* drawn into the orbit of a lovable and intimate other."[17] And the social psychologists Gary Sherman and Jonathan Haidt go so far as to consider the cuteness response a "moral emotion" par excellence: a "direct releaser of human sociality" that draws cute entities into our circle of moral concern—concern for the welfare of others— which is, in turn, a condition for maximizing "caring, altruism, and prosocial behavior towards strangers and towards animals."[18]

In any event, the spirit of condemnation— which is increasingly all the rage in the West—will not, in the case of Cute, as in so much else, enrich our insight, but will rather impoverish it. And so my aim here is to resist the urge to censure the craze for Cute— and instead to seek a wider understanding of this fascinating phenomenon and the diverse roles it plays in today's world.

2

Spooked in the Garden of Eden

At first glance, Cute is indeed all about evoking a garden of innocence in which childlike qualities arouse deliciously protective feelings in its viewers and imbue them with contentment and solace. Cute cues include behavior that appears helpless, harmless, charming, and yielding, and anatomical features such as outsize heads, protruding foreheads, saucerlike eyes, retreating chins, and clumsy gaits.

Perhaps, as the great scholar of animal behavior, Konrad Lorenz, suggested in 1943, our response to these sorts of cues evolved to motivate us to give our offspring the extensive care and nurture that they need to prosper.[1] According to Lorenz, human adults are hardwired with such responsiveness, which we have inherited from our evolutionary ancestors. Moreover, he claimed, the same visual cues can arouse us to equally intense—or possibly more intense—caregiving when we encounter them in exaggerated and distilled form in animals, such as birds and puppies, and even in dummy models, such as dolls and teddy bears. Thus we will want to pet, cuddle, and gush over the rounder, softer profiles in the left column of figure 2.1—whereas the more angular heads in the right column will leave us cold.

On this basis, we would find anything cute that exhibits such morphological and behavioral cues, even if it doesn't exactly resemble human or animal forms. And our mania for Cute would be grounded in an urge to nurture, or else to escape into the reassuring world of the powerless and the innocent: to flee to safety and simplicity. Such powerlessness will arouse tender care—or, in

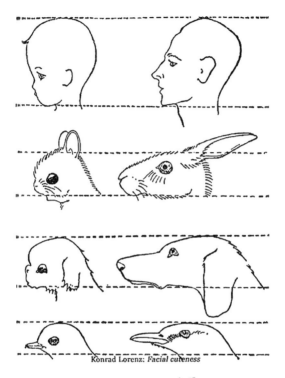

Konrad Lorenz: *Facial cuteness*

FIG. 2.1 Features common to different species (cute cues) that evoke the caregiving response, according to Konrad Lorenz. Konrad Lorenz, *Studies in Animal and Human Behaviour,* vol. 2, trans. Robert Martin (Cambridge, Mass.: Harvard University Press), copyright © 1971 by Konrad Lorenz.

a perversion of our feeling of power over the vulnerable and helpless, impulses to sadism. It will evoke protectiveness or perversity, or some fetishistic combination of the two.

Either way, we feel the solace of the cocoon. We revel in release from helplessness in front of the unpredictable and often violent world of everyday life, where we have little control over our destiny. We crave the safety and simplicity of an enclosed and familiar space where we are in charge and where we are faced with an object that is innocent in every sense: an object that is good, naive, gentle—and free from greed, cynicism, cruelty, hatred, and violent intent.

❖

And yet, I am suggesting, this charming world of the helpless and harmless represents just one end of the great spectrum that is Cute. And so it misses a more obscure, intractable, and challenging world that increasingly comes into view as we move along the spectrum and that is maximally expressed at its other end.

Those charming qualities that conjure an existence of perfect innocence, pliancy, and dependence, unburdened by contradiction and complexity, are what we might call "sweet"—the qualities to which *mignon* in French and *Süss* in German refer. Here we also find kittens playing with balls of yarn, babies with "dimpled knees and round faces with bright, wide-open eyes and blemishless skin,"[2] and the puppy with kindly eyes, drooping ears, and soft fur (see fig. 2.2).

The further we progress away from the purely sweet end of the Cute spectrum, however, the more the characteristics and proportions of the Sweet become distorted into—or tinged by—something unsafe, elusive, alienated, artful, menacing, knowing, apprehensive, absurdist, resilient. In other words, things become more poignantly or uncannily cute the more such qualities are seen to saturate sweetness: the more they pervade the luminous, unthreatening, artless, familiar,

FIG. 2.2 The purely sweet end of the Cute spectrum. Wikimedia Commons, uploaded by Ron Clausen.

wholesome, available, open, vulnerable nature of the Sweet. So that it comes to seem unknowing and yet knowing, perfectly formed and yet also deformed, familiar and unfamiliar, comforting and also discomforting, intimate and untouchable, innocuous and garish. All in a playful way. And all without allowing us, the viewer, to know whether these seeming opposites are in tension or in harmony.

This is the world that is overlooked by conventional views of Cute as merely innocent, playful, guileless, helpless. It is a world that, far from being only familiar and unthreatening, is also unfamiliar and menacing—indeed, that involves a dialogue between the familiar and unfamiliar, the unthreatening and the menacing, the present and the withdrawn, the visible and the invisible. Which is why the far end of the Cute spectrum—what I will call "uncanny Cute"—is for adults and children older than six or seven, whereas the sweet end is for all ages, toddlers included. Toddlers wouldn't get, or need, uncanny Cute. They want just the comforting teddy bear, complete with an ample tummy, full limbs, and large button eyes, rather than the deformed Hello Kitty: mouthless, voiceless, fingerless, and having only dots for eyes and nose.

Heidi the cross-eyed opossum is a knock-out partly because she is a fabulously cuddly marsupial, but also because she is afflicted with painful vulnerability: there is a drop of horror in her innocence. E.T., the Extra-Terrestrial, is both childlike, with its bulbous forehead, large eyes, and unjaded demeanor, and at the same time sadly aged, with its wrinkled skin, gangly limbs, and appearance of having experienced suffering.[3] As Daniel Harris remarks, Winnie the Pooh is perhaps most charming when his snout is stuck painfully in a honey pot. Disney's 101 Dalmatians are never more adorable than when "collapsing in double splits and sprawling across the ice." "Little Mutt" is a teddy bear with an injured leg, which is designed to be all the cuter for having been fitted with an orthopedic boot. The Cabbage Patch Kids, a craze in the United States back in the 1980s—those "ugly little dolls that have somehow seized the heart of the nation," as the *New York Times* called them—succeeded not despite being ugly but because of it. And So Shy Sherri, with her swollen ankles and pigeon-toed feet, is endearing precisely as an "anatomical disaster."[4]

Cute compels us, not because of such vulnerabilities, but because we stumble across them in what we expect to be a Garden of Eden.

❖

This brings us to the essence of all Cute that isn't merely sweet—and the key to its hypnotic power: its teasing indeterminacy. Not an indeterminacy that hesitates but one that is forthright—that announces all sides of its nature openly, shamelessly, and often playfully or self-deprecatingly. This is an indeterminacy that, like E.T. or *Balloon Dog*, makes the grotesque—the, to us, weirdly distorted—charming and the charming grotesque; one that takes the sting out of danger and puts the sting into safety, so that both the grotesque and the charming, the danger and the safety, seem not quite real; one that makes the familiar unfamiliar and the unfamiliar familiar, thus inducing that powerful sense of the uncanny described by Sigmund Freud, to which I will return later.[5] Indeed, E.T. calls to mind Konrad Lorenz's observation that there is a threshold where sweet features morph into eeriness—a threshold that Lorenz identifies with the Kewpie doll, which

FIG. 2.3 E.T.—the Extra-Terrestrial (1982). AF archive / Alamy Stock Photo.

"represents the maximum possible exaggeration of the proportions between cranium and face which perception can tolerate without switching our response from the sweet baby to that elicited by the eerie monster."[6] (See fig. 2.3.)

Thus to see the cuteness response as evoked mainly by familiar, unthreatening objects is to capture chiefly the sweet end of the spectrum. If power over familiar objects—and their implicit power over us insofar as we need them—were all that there was to Cute, it would lack much of its sway. As we have seen with E.T. and Hello Kitty and *Balloon Dog*, among many other examples that could be given, Cute is mesmerizing precisely because it moves mercurially between familiarity and unfamiliarity, homey and alienated, light and dark, delight and sorrow, harmlessness and menace, harmony and dissonance, shapen and misshapen, innocence and wisdom, neediness and self-sufficiency, vulnerability and resilience, the imaginary and the real, and even the human and the inhuman (or nonhuman), without ever taking a clear stand. Without even *seeking* a resolution of these tensions.

And, crucially, without heaviness. A grave stance—seriousness, shame, pomposity, anger, condemnation, blame, and their ilk—would destroy Cute instantly, and turn us from doting on its object to despising it. Even when a cute object looks lifeless, or totally passive, it feels cutest when we see it to be playing dead. Cute works best if its distortions and deformations have levity. Easygoing humor, outrageousness, zaniness—these give Cute its edge, its third dimension.

3

Cute as an Uncertainty Principle

Since ancient times, irresolvable ambivalence has fascinated as well as unnerved—or fascinated because it has unnerved. Transgression of familiar categories is not a monopoly of the modern or postmodern spirit.

The hermaphrodite is, historically, one such figure of ambivalence. It has a central place in mythology, where it is often seen as a disquieting corruption of the natural order. In Ovid's telling of the story of the teenage god Hermaphroditus, son of

Hermes and Aphrodite (respectively the thieving messenger of the gods and the goddess of love), the young man becomes half-woman as a result of spurning the advances of the water nymph Salmacis by an enchanted lake. Desperate to ensnare him, Salmacis prays to the gods to fuse their bodies forever. Finding Hermaphroditus swimming in the lake she jumps in after him and clings to him until they become one body that seems "to have no sex and yet to have both." Condemned to this eternal ambivalence, Hermaphroditus, in his turn, begs his parents to make every other man who swims in the lake become only a half-man. As Ovid tells us, Hermes and Aphrodite duly "heard the prayer of their two-formed son, and charged the waters with that uncanny power."[1]

Like many of our contemporary depictions of Cute, Ovid's tale speaks of a tortured, helpless, and indeterminate state of being—of timeless human fascination with the transgressive-uncanny.

❖

I do not know whether Cute, as we experience it today, appealed as strongly to distant ages as it does to ours—indeed as it has done, in particular, since the end of the Second World War and, above all, since the 1960s in the West and the 1970s in Japan. In, say, Imperial Rome of the second century BCE, or Renaissance Florence of the fifteenth century, or Rococo Venice of the eighteenth century, did putti and small animals and children evoke the kind of emotion and judgment that today we call Cute? Even if figures, real or fictional, existed that bore the qualities now ascribed to Cute, was this sensibility thematized, and did a word exist to denote it?

As I will suggest in chapter 9, Cute is, among other things, a new expression of an ancient sensibility, namely the monstrous; a contemporary way of giving voice to the ancient trope of the monstrous hybrid. Though another manifestation, or at least near neighbor, of the monstrous—namely, the grotesque or the fantastic—which Vasari described as "very ridiculous and licentious,"[2] has been thematized since the Italian Renaissance, Cute is of much more recent origin, whether as a way of being or as a form of self-identity. The term seems to make its debut no earlier than the eighteenth century—perhaps not surprisingly, as this is the century in which "aesthetics" as a self-consciously distinct philosophical discipline emerges, along with the new categories it spawns such as "the Sublime" and, according to Susan Sontag, "Camp."[3] But "Cute" becomes widely used, along with the related but different sensibility of "Kitsch,"[4] only from around the middle of the nineteenth century.

Indeed, this is just the time at which Cute begins to be big business. An early pioneer of commercial cuteness was the exotically named Phineas Taylor Barnum, an American who detected an emerging market for so-called baby shows, in which mothers and their children were put on public display. The first of these, held in 1855 at the American

Museum on New York's Broadway, attracted over sixty thousand viewers and one hundred and forty-three contestants. Though other shows soon followed, the craze was, from the outset, not without its critics, many of whom deemed unacceptably crass the public flaunting of what they held should be a private relationship between mother and child: "There is something intrinsically revolting," remarked one woman, "in this attempt to force aside the veil which screens and protects the chaste matron, where she and her 'pretty brood' within the sanctuary of home are exempt from the rude gaze of a prying curiosity."[5]

Undeterred, the savvy Barnum then turned his attention to Charles Stratton, a four-year-old who was only twenty inches tall when he was hired to be an "exhibit" at the American Museum, and whom he branded "General Tom Thumb" after the English fairy-tale character who was the size of an adult's thumb and who, by the mid-nineteenth century, had become a staple of nursery stories. At the age of only six, General Tom Thumb became a celebrity in America—and then internationally, being received by European royalty and performing in London and elsewhere to packed houses. And in 1862, Barnum arranged his engagement—he was now twenty-four years old and all of thirty-one inches high—to the "smallest woman in the world," the twenty-one-year-old Lavinia Warren Bump, herself thirty-two inches tall. Their marriage was attended by thousands, gifts were sent by President Lincoln and a host of America's wealthiest families, and the *New York Times*, reporting the event in breathless detail, averred that on this "most momentous" occasion, a man as well known as Louis Napoleon Bonaparte betrothed himself to "The Queen of Beauty"[6] (see fig. 3.1). Cuteness, albeit in an embodiment that would be anathema today, was coming into its own.

❖

This emergence of Cute "as a common term of evaluation and formally recognizable style

FIG. 3.1 Tom Thumb and Lavinia Warren Bump get married at New York's Grace Church, February 1863. Strattons, G.W.M. Nutt, and Minnie Warren (Wedding Party). Mathew Brady Studio (1863, printed later). Modern albumen print from wet plate collodion negative. National Portrait Gallery, Smithsonian Institution; Meserve Collection.

in the industrial nineteenth century United States" goes together, according to Sianne Ngai, with the "ideological consolidation of the middle class home as a feminized space supposedly organized primarily around commodities and consumption."[7] Thus cuteness is "an adoration of the commodity"—generally experienced as less powerful than me, its viewer—an adoration "in which I want to be as intimate with or physically close to it as possible."[8] And the commercial success of Cute is driven by nascent mass consumer culture (just as Kitsch, in the view of the art critic Clement Greenberg, is a product of the Industrial Revolution), becoming ever more marked with the dawn of the twentieth century, and accelerating further just after the First World War when "'cute' toys, in the strong sense of denoting an aesthetic of accentuated helplessness and vulnerability, began appearing in the United States in mass quantities."[9]

Surprisingly, perhaps, there have been only two sorts of definition of Cute since the earliest known use of the word, around 1731.

The first is a shortening of "acute" and means "sharp, quick witted"[10] as well as "clever or shrewd, often in an underhanded manner."[11] The second definition, which emerges in the 1830s, gives Cute an almost opposite meaning: innocent, attractive, and charming, especially in a childlike way. But, as I have suggested, the latter denotes little more than the "sweet" end of the spectrum.

If, however, we fuse these two distinct definitions together, like Hermaphroditus and Salmacis, we begin to do justice to Cute's fuller meaning: to, precisely, its ambivalences. Innocent cunning. Cunning innocence.

And Cute as innocent cunning is just what we start to see in the early twentieth century. Indeed, it is perfectly exemplified by that icon of 1930s cuteness, the child movie star Shirley Temple, "America's Sweetheart," whose extraordinary film career starts at only age five. The new mania for cute kids was impelling thousands of parents to send their toddlers to dancing school, but few had Shirley Temple's many-sided talents for dancing, singing, and acting—and, above all, for embodying the "angelic imp." For, as Gary Cross emphasizes, "the 'cuteness' of Shirley was not narrowly defined; an essential part of her appeal was the fact that her image slid between the naïve/dependent and the wise/vital," epitomized by her "flirtatious innocence." The whole point of the impish angel is that she is a nymphet "wilfully but naively on the moral boundary."[12] In other words: she is by no means merely sweet.

Today, Cute is, I suggest, one of the largely unspoken ways in which we experience the impossibility of pure innocence and, beyond that, the insuperable indeterminacy of human nature. Adult/child, knowing/naive, feminine/masculine, good/bad, knowable/unknowable—the sharpness of these dichotomies breaks down under the aspect of Cute. Perhaps this is why cute objects so often lack clear identities, for example, in respect of gender, morality, knowability, age, and indeed ethnicity. And we need a new way of looking at it that reflects this.

❖

In everyday life, uncannily cute people don't behave in a purely sweet way. They desperately want to be noticed but not to be fussed over, to be cared for but not to be cocooned. They feel alien and alienated—but leave us unsure whether and how to rescue them. Whereas the sweet straightforwardly invite rescue, fuss, cocooning. (And it is worth remarking, in passing, that if we are inclined to doubt whether people can be cute, we will see in chapter 5, when we consider contemporary Japan, how not just individuals but an entire national spirit can be suffused by Cute—indeed, how it has come to govern both Japan's perception of itself and the face it shows to the world.)

In addition, the uncannily cute are knowing—and not only innocent in the manner of the Sweet. In particular, they are intensely aware of relations of power. The old definition of cute as shrewd or clever, far from being unrelated to the sense I am suggesting, is an excellent guide to precisely this knowingness. To see Cute as necessarily innocent is so one-sided as to be outright wrong.

As well as being knowing, such cute people long to be known and recognized—and, true to their unpindownability, then to hide. They want you formally to adopt them, but they are ever vigilant to threats to their independence, the worst of which is any attempt to force them to abandon their undetermined positions and take a stand or, almost as bad, to inhabit a world of solemnity and gravity. Hiding and playing powerless are crucial to their identity, which is itself never resolved, never decided. In fact, they use their vulnerability to tease and manipulate. Their very nature poses the old question: Who really has the power—the master or the slave?

The master's power is the more obvious: the slave depends on him for food, freedom, shelter, maybe even for life itself. The master can turn the slave into a mere instrument, into a nonperson. But, to adapt a famous argument of the German philosopher Georg Wilhelm Friedrich Hegel (1770-1831), the slave's power might be the more fundamental. For the master's very identity depends on the slave's existence; he needs the slave's work and life to be at his disposal in order to think of himself as a master—in order to be the sort of person he is. More than that: he needs the slave to *recognize* his status as a slave—as dependent on the master for freedom and income; as owing the master his work, his submission, indeed his very life—in order to feel a master. And if he wants to get such recognition from the slave, he needs to preserve—in other words, to recognize—the slave's humanity; he isn't free to annul the slave's dignity altogether, to turn him into a mere object. For though an object can be exploited, it cannot offer recognition, which, Hegel says, is a fundamental human need, vital to the very possibility of individual identity and freedom. Were, therefore, the master to discover that he had at his disposal a lifeless robot, he would no longer feel a *master*.[13]

The uncannily cute can't help reminding us that in our intimate relations we often don't know who really has the upper hand. They invite you to toy with them and then visit their part feigned, part genuine fury on you for doing so. They enjoy being on the receiving end of power—but only if it is playful; any serious attempt to strong-arm them or actually to master them will be rejected. They draw you in and then spit you out— charmingly. One moment they behave like a slave and refuse all autonomy, presenting themselves as your plaything; the next, they behave as a master, willfully dictating the terms of their relations with you.

It is therefore deeply one-sided at best, and can simply be wrong, to claim that "the process of conveying cuteness to the viewer disempowers its objects, forcing them into ridiculous situations and making them appear more ignorant and vulnerable than they really are."[14] Quite the opposite: the process of conveying cuteness to the viewer potentially *empowers* the cute by allowing them to play with the viewer's sense of her own power, now painting her into a dominant pose, now sowing uncertainty about who is really in charge, now making her realize that the cute one's surrender is actually a way of entrapping her, now making demands for care or protection from her.

❖

And cuteness can play not only with the question of who really has power but also with another, perhaps more fundamental question: How much does power matter? The cute might indeed be passive and vulnerable—and yet they might also be resistant to manipulation, impervious to force, unmoved by the control of their viewers. What is the viewer to do then with his "power"? What's the point of being in the dominant position? To what end the satisfaction in lording it over those one takes to be helpless? In short: the vulnerability, alleged or real, of the cute doesn't only draw attention to inequalities of power; crucially it also questions their very purpose and effect.

For at least a century and a half, from the mid-nineteenth to the early twenty-first—from Nietzsche to Foucault and beyond—power has been widely taken to be the key to understanding human relations, and even life itself. Love, sex, morals, art-making, social structures, institutions, gender relations, concepts, standards of taste—all these have been seen as expressions of the power of those who define and partake in them. For Nietzsche, "life itself is *will to power*"—indeed, we inhabit "a world whose essence is will to power."[15] Even selflessness, compassion, and humility can serve the function of securing power for the individual—over others; over life. For Foucault, all social institutions and practices are to be understood in terms of the power relations that constitute them, so that even what are taken to be hard-won freedoms, such as sexual liberation or women's emancipation, can be, for him, no genuine liberation but rather a fresh expression of society's surveillance and control of "the life of the species."[16]

Cute doesn't, and perhaps can't, overturn this now dominant paradigm. And as we will see in chapter 13, it is unsuited to pursuing such clear ends as rebutting or replacing a paradigm. Instead, Cute unsettles the habitual by toying with it from a position of playful vulnerability. It lightheartedly probes the established ways in which we invoke power to order our priorities and to understand who we are.

At the same time, whether behaving as slave or master, or as both, the cute always seem blameless. This is one of their signature features: neither blame nor responsibility can attach to them (though it can of course attach to their noncute traits). Not because they explicitly refuse responsibility, or are taken to do so; nor because they are too helpless and childlike to assume it. Rather, Cute has no relation—its very makeup is alien—to responsibility. It is amoral, unconcerned with morality—as if unaware of conventional classifications of good and bad. Its tremendous attractiveness to our age—and its tremendous danger—is that it secures a space that seems neither moral nor immoral. Within Cute, questions of morality feel out of place.

Which is why we cannot assume that Cute, or attraction to it, can only manifest regression to infantile innocence. Sweet *is* infantile, but at the other end of the spectrum, uncanny Cute is experienced. It is aware of the horrors of the world—indeed, to an extent it embodies them—but it doesn't look to morality to do anything about them. You can be sweet with barely any experience—as babies are. So when Lorenz describes those physical and behavioral features of an infant that evoke an adult's caregiving response, he is depicting only the Sweet.

Indeed, uncanny cuteness seems to have tasted, seen, and metabolized much bitter experience. Its strength—even genius—is to feed on bitterness and yet not to manifest bitterness. It might appear a little cruel, but it is not resentful. It might be a tad aggressive, but it is not vengeful.

All of this only hints at the complexity of Cute. Uncanny cuteness has a hinterland, often seen through a glass darkly; Sweet is immediate, translucent, never withholding of itself.

4

Mickey Mouse and the Cuteness Continuum

Much of the time, we prefer to huddle at the sweet end of the spectrum, doting on those objects conventionally regarded as cute. Uncanny cuteness, which gradually comes into view as we move along the spectrum away from Sweet and is maximal at its other end, though beguiling, unnerves us. And so we veer away from it towards the simpler hues of the infantile—towards those qualities identified by Konrad Lorenz:

- a head large in relation to the body;
- an outsize, protruding forehead;

- large eyes set relatively low in the head, compared with adults (in adult humans, the eyes are positioned about halfway down the head; in infants, they are about two-thirds of the way down);
- round, bulging cheeks;
- plump, rounded body shape;
- short and thick extremities;
- soft body surfaces that are pleasurable to touch; and
- helpless and clumsy movements.[1]

The evolutionary biologist Stephen Jay Gould identifies a strange flight towards just such infantility in the development of Mickey Mouse over the half-century from the late 1920s to the late 1970s. We think of Mickey as epitomizing many of these childlike features—and, in tune with this anatomy, as a perfectly sweet-natured, straight-talking little creature whose pluckiness and self-reliance somehow win out in a world of constant danger.

But he wasn't always thus. In his early years his head, forehead, and eyes had all

been more adult—that is, more proportion-
ate to the rest of his body; his ears had been
farther forward, and his legs, arms, and
nose straighter and more tapered. Behav-
iorally, he had often been a thoroughly un-
principled go-getter, "a rambunctious, even
slightly sadistic fellow."[2] He strutted rather
than waddled and courted trouble rather
than avoiding it. Far from being a goody
two-shoes who rescues the vulnerable, respects his fellows, and sees off creatures
of ill will, he has a go at the weak, messes
with their privates, and isn't lacking a few
evil intentions himself. In his debut performance in *Steamboat Willie* (1928), he and
Minnie

> pummel, squeeze, and twist the animals
> on board to produce a rousing chorus of
> "Turkey in the Straw." They honk a duck
> with a tight embrace, crank a goat's tail,
> tweak a pig's nipples, bang cow's teeth
> as a stand-in xylophone, and play bag-
> pipe on her udder.[3]

Within just over a decade, and soon after the outbreak of the Second World War, the obnoxious Mickey of *Steamboat Willie* is transformed from a tweaker of pigs' nipples into an altogether more disciplined mouse (he gets punished for insubordination as the Sorcerer's Apprentice in the 1940 cartoon *Fantasia*). By 1953 he is seen as a placid fisherman, unable or unwilling to subdue even a squirting clam, and not long after that he ends up as the Mickey known to us today: the benevolent host and denizen of a magic kingdom (see fig. 4.1).[4]

❖

Why did Mickey's creators come to direct his evolution in precisely the opposite way to normal development—in other words backwards, to childhood? Why did Walt Disney reportedly order his animators to change tack and "keep it cute!"?[5] One might think that it was because Mickey needed to become respectable once he had made it as an American national figure[6]—that a great and

FIG. 4.1 Mickey Mouse's flight towards infantility over fifty years (left to right). As Mickey became increasingly well behaved, his appearance became more youthful. His relative head size increased, as did his eyes and his cranium—all traits of juvenility. © The Walt Disney Archives.

God-fearing people couldn't fall in love with and expose its young to an udder-sucking sadist. He had to have a moral makeover and embody the Anglo-Protestant ethic of his nation rather than mock it. He had to be wholesome, irreproachable, virtuous, reliable. He had to be a mouse of his word.

But, Gould speculates, there could be another motive for Mickey's "progressive juvenalization."[7] His creators might have found it profitable for him to appeal to something deeper than American morality: humanity's instinct to nurture its young. For, as Lorenz had shown, this could be displaced onto any number of cute objects, whether living or not, that mimic the features of infancy. The shapes that Mickey acquired as he shed his offensive behavior—a more bulbous head, larger eyes, and a bigger cranial vault—were just the sorts of cues that Lorenz had identified as "innate releasing mechanisms"[8] of humans' caregiving response to their young.

Is that, however, the real reason for Mickey's reverse evolution at just this historical moment, shortly after the outbreak of the Second World War? Both the moral wholesomeness explanation and Gould's evolutionary speculation miss obvious points: America's basic ethic hadn't changed in the fifty years since Mickey was first created. Nor had the timeless instinct of human beings to nurture their young suddenly become more potent or self-conscious. Something else—something genuinely novel—must have been afoot to which the shrewd Walt Disney had responded, whether consciously or not.

What was new was the unsurpassed horrors of the two world wars—or rather people's refusal to tolerate the horrors of war any longer: their determination finally to create a world free of lethal enmity between nations, a world safe for humanity's gentler instincts. The First World War, terrible though it had been, hadn't yet achieved this new will. It was only after the Second that Americans, Europeans, and, crucially, Japanese became seized by revulsion for violence and cruelty; by overwhelming desire for a world of innocence and gentleness and cooperation, in which terrible suffering would be abolished and human aggression finally disarmed.

Japan and most of Western Europe abjured power politics abroad and created welfare states at home. America emerged from the war as the strongest nation in the world and perhaps in all human history, but it too was not immune to yearning for peaceful cooperation—for safety and order achieved not through being threatening but through being unthreatening. Indeed, it played a leading role in creating, developing, and encouraging the great institutions of international cooperation that arose out of that war—the International Monetary Fund, the World Bank, the European Community (later the European Union), the United Nations—all of which were in many ways inspired by the same feelings as the new, tamer Mickey Mouse.

Cuteness might seem a far cry from the fusty facelessness of the IMF, the UN, or the EU; but, like them, the cult of Cute expressed the dominant hope of the age: the hope that everything peaceful and unifying and cooperative and homely in human nature could prevail; that might isn't necessarily right; that the instincts of mutual protection and nurturing and altruism could be celebrated; that human community could attain a new golden age; that the vision of "perpetual peace," given its greatest expression by the

eighteenth-century Enlightenment philosopher Immanuel Kant, might indeed be realized between nations that share fundamental
interests and values. Like those vast bureau-
cracies, the cult of Cute was in no small part
catalyzed by fear of the ever-present threat of
violence in the rivalry of nations as of individuals. And that fear evinced the other side
of Cute: awareness of the dark, the apprehensive, and the vulnerable. Dark, apprehensive,
vulnerable, and yet—true to the essence of
Cute—defiant, resilient, and lighthearted.

5

Kawaii: The New Japanese Imperium

If the violence of war inspires an explosion of Cute in victorious America, how much truer this is in vanquished Japan. Bombed into unconditional surrender by the United States in August 1945 with atom bombs given the perversely harmless (cute?) names of "Little Boy" and "Fat Man," and then, in short order, facing three heavily armed communist neighbors—Soviet Russia, China, and North Korea—the last two of which are filled with loathing for Japan's recent cruelty to their peoples, the country devotes itself to elaborating a way of being—including an aesthetic—that is, and is seen to be, diametrically opposed to its erstwhile warrior instincts. But that is, nonetheless, like most powerful ways of being, nourished by a long heritage.

At first, humility is the name of the game. Japan has to rebuild its cities, its economy, and the trust of its American conquerors as well as of other wartime enemies. Then, from as early as the mid-1960s, only twenty years after total defeat, with these tasks completed or well under way, there is room, alongside the relentless striving after industrial supremacy, for more confident, relaxed, and even rebellious moods—in the widest sense of the word "mood": a way of being in the world, a mode of attunement to it, such that it shows up to us or is disclosed to us in a certain way, as, for Martin Heidegger, anxiety is paradigmatically a mood ("Stimmung" in German).[1] And crucially: despite violent interludes, such as the student riots of the 1960s, these moods are, for the most part, not overtly violent.

From the early 1970s, one such mood bursts onto the scene, catalyzed by—and at first expressed almost exclusively in—the "girl culture" of the *shōjo*: young, often adolescent, unmarried females;[2] then taken up by women of various ages; and after the late 1980s, embraced by increasing numbers of young men for whom, according to Sharon Kinsella, "cute fashion represents freedom and an escape from the pressure of social expectations and regulations," and who "fetishize young women—either real girl friends or syrupy sweet little girl heroines depicted in Lolita complex comic books for adolescent boys."[3] This mood is *kawaii*, which—as Takashi Murakami, among other Japanese artists and scholars, agrees—more or less translates as "cute," and which, already in 1992, was called "the most widely used, widely loved, habitual word in modern living Japanese."[4]

As a sensibility, *kawaii* goes beyond its first postwar manifestation as helpless and vulnerable cues that pervade Japanese girl culture, and—as we will see in the art of Murakami,

Nara, and Miyazaki, for example—becomes much more richly indeterminate. To portray oneself as *kawaii*, in this richer sense, is to appear not just vulnerable and in need of protection but also defiantly self-sufficient; to be not just unthreatening (to outsiders and, crucially for postwar Japan, in its perception of *itself*) but also subtly ruthless about one's own preservation; to parade one's powerlessness and yet to be cheerful and even amused by it; to be predictable and yet remain mercurial; to be literal and also ironical; to be transparent and yet to wear successions of masks; to be harmony-loving and yet to be zany, deformed, jarring. And, not least, to allow oneself a whiff of melancholy—but again, in a lighthearted way.

It's a big jump in self-conception from Samurai to Cute, but it perfectly suits Japan's historical position after the disaster of militarism. Where, today, Germany does remorse, Japan does Cute. Not straightforward Sweet, which would look pitiful; but rather the altogether more robust and playful, more indirect and opaque spirit of Cute—a spirit that can magically make vanish everything that is aggressive and threatening.

And so, Cute in Japan is far from merely light escapism into "feminized" self-images and social networks; or into infantile or adolescent behaviors, trinkets, cartoons, and language codes. It is a whole world, a parallel universe. And it allows the country to show a face to foreigners—and, most importantly, to itself—that is at once reassuring and quirky, transparent and yet baffling.

Or more than a face: Cute has become so much a part of the Japanese spirit, as it is manifested today, that outer face has become inner reality. *Tatemae*, how you show yourself to others, or how you think they want to see or hear you, has, in this respect, gone a long way to becoming *honne*, how you actually feel.

Sharon Kinsella vividly describes—though perhaps with one-sided emphasis on the infantile dimension of Cute—how *kawaii* is much more than just possessing or fawning over cute things. In addition, and perhaps most importantly, it is "about 'becoming' the cute object itself." Speaking of the tremendous growth of the craze in the 1990s, she says:

> Young Japanese, especially women, purchased cute accessories and filled their rooms, cars, desks at work, and handbags with sweet paraphernalia as a way of surrounding themselves by cuteness, to the point where they felt transformed and could enter this cute-only world themselves. Being cute meant behaving childlike—which involved an act of self-mutilation, posing with pigeon toes, pulling wide-eyed innocent expressions, dieting, acting stupid, and essentially denying the existence of the wealth of insights, feelings, and humour that maturity brings with it. In cute culture, young people became popular according to their apparent weakness, dependence and inability, rather than because of their strengths and capabilities.[5]

Cute has gone so far to becoming *honne*, how one feels, that becoming cute is not just an act, a performance, or a set of signs that bond people socially; it pervades the soul of the nation in a way that would not be easy to throw off.

To the extent, laments the artist Takashi Murakami—one of Japan's iconic makers, and also excoriators, of Cute—that the country has "emasculated," indeed "castrated" itself as a direct result of Hiroshima and Nagasaki—in order, we can infer from his writing, never again to invite a nuclear attack. "*Kawaii* (cute) culture has become a living entity that pervades everything" in contemporary Japan, Murakami writes in a book entitled *Little Boy*, the name of the Hiroshima bomb, which accompanied an exhibition of his work in 2005:

> It is a utopian society as fully regulated as the science-fiction world George Orwell envisioned in 1984: comfortable, happy, fashionable—a world nearly devoid of discriminatory

impulses. . . . These monotonous ruins of a nation-state, which arrived on the heels of an American puppet government, have been perfectly realized in the name of capitalism. . . . When *kawaii, hetare* (loser), and *yurui* (loose or lethargic) characters smile wanly or stare vacantly, people around the world should recognize a gradually fusing, happy heart. It should be possible to find the kernels of our future by examining how indigenous Japanese imagery and aesthetics changed and accelerated after the war, solidifying into their current forms.

And he concludes: "We Japanese still embody 'Little Boy.'"[6]

❖

And so, from the early 1970s, Cute storms the land, becoming an ever more prominent language of advertisements, government exhortations, safety warnings, manga, and consumer goods from mobile phones to lunch boxes and calendars. It is embraced not just by young people, male and female, in their teens and twenties, but also by public officials, sales assistants, airlines, banks, insurance companies, and even the operators of bulldozers, whose cabs are often adorned with cute stickers. The "pocket monsters" that populate the play world of Pokémon, with its video games, movies, comic books, toy merchandise, and card series, become global ambassadors for Japanese Cute. Indeed, in 2008, Japan's Ministry of Foreign Affairs designated a robotic cat character with no ears called Doraemon as the country's "cartoon culture ambassador," swiftly followed in 2009 by the government's appointment of three human Ambassadors of Cute (*kawaii taishi*),[7] one dressed as a miniskirted schoolgirl, another as a Victorian doll in pastel frills, representing so-called Lolita fashion, and the third in a polka dot shirt with a bunny print (see fig. 5.1).

67

FIG. 5.1 The Japanese government's official Ambassadors of Cute (2009). Michael Caronna / Reuters Pictures.

Unsurprisingly, the Japanese armed forces, too, have bedecked themselves in Cute. The army has used "an incongruous mix of doe-eyed anime waifs and camouflaged soldiers for its recruitment posters"; anti-missile defenses on warships might be "anthropomorphized into a bunny rabbit, complete with mortar tubes for ears"[8] in order to demonstrate their capabilities and combat-readiness to members

FIG. 5.2 A Japanese anti-tank attack helicopter (2013). © Monsieur Ashiya / Flickr, uploaded under an Attribution-NonCommercial-ShareAlike 2.0 Generic (CC BY-NC-SA 2.0) license.

of the public; and anti-tank attack helicopters have been seen festooned with anime-style cute girl cartoons (see fig. 5.2).

As the twenty-first century got under way, even the intensely sensitive matter of World War Two battleships might be recast as *kawaii*. In the hugely popular video game and anime franchise "Combined Fleet Girls Collection," battleships are portrayed "as cute young girls clad in revealing uniforms." Though in reality many of the ships that these girls symbolize sank with the loss of thousands of lives, they now became occasions for teen dramas, which played out at a naval base "amidst sorties against undersea invaders."[9]

❖

And yet it would be wrong to see *kawaii* as a fetishistic surrender aesthetic that advertises nothing but passivity and harmlessness—a reassuring way of embellishing and entrenching national self-enfeeblement. *Kawaii* doesn't just eviscerate Japan of internal and external violence. It also does the very opposite: it allows violence to be expressed in an unsolemn, unthreatening way. As well as extirpating aggression, Cute also sublimates it.

Here again, it is the opposite to the spirit of Samurai. We see this in the work of artists like Yoshitomo Nara, Aya Takano, Chiho Aoshima, and Minako Nishiyama—as well as of Murakami himself. In many of their works, irony and a light touch burnish violence with Cute.

Thus Nara's images of isolated and dejected children seem strangely harmless, though they might be expected to arouse unqualified disgust—not least in today's West, where childhood has, over the last century, come to be regarded as sacred. Indeed Nara's work commands a "large international community of fans, many of them young women."[10] His children's underlying despair is palpable and distressing; yet unlike extreme despair, it isn't imprisoned in hopelessness, nor does it obviously cry out to be rescued. On the contrary, their innocence is juxtaposed to a knowingness, defiance, and even flippancy about their predicament. Vulnerability coexists with resilience. To an indeterminate degree some of them seem to be at least partially in control of their vulnerability, acting their passivity, even ironizing it, as if to say to their viewers: "Well, if this is what *you* want and need, then here it is. Let me not only be powerless but play powerless for you; it doesn't bother me." In other words, they seem both to be vulnerable and to act vulnerable.

To that extent, Nara's children embody both original meanings of "cute": naive and savvy. Where they evince a note of anger it doesn't seem to assume the straightforward fury that can be fomented by pure despair. It is more indeterminate—and more deadpan sardonic—than that: once again, in the manner of Cute, unpindownable. In such ways, his image *This Is How It Feels When Your Word Means Nothing At All* is ominous but far from totally desolate; and the longer we dwell on it, as well as on the words "KIDS DON'T KNOW," the more uncertain we become about how unknowing and vulnerable, angry and despondent this kid really is. And so the harder straightforward outrage seems to be (see fig. 5.3).

At times, Nara's children seem to fight back—or, again, in his masterful deployment of uncertainty, appear to be about to do so; or perhaps to feign, or to mock, fighting back. Even when they don't hold knives and other

FIG. 5.3 Yoshitomo Nara, *This Is How It Feels When Your Word Means Nothing At All* (1995). Acrylic on canvas, 19.88 × 15.55 in. (50.5 × 39.5 cm). Photograph courtesy the artist. © Yoshitomo Nara, courtesy Pace Gallery.

FIG. 5.4 Yoshitomo Nara, *Fight It Out* (2002). Colored pencil on paper (envelope), 15 × 9 in. (37.5 × 24 cm). Photograph courtesy the artist. © Yoshitomo Nara, courtesy Pace Gallery.

obvious instruments of power or violence, they perfectly exemplify my question in chapter 3: Who, in the relationship of the cute to their spectators, holds the balance of power? Is it necessarily the spectator? Indeed, they force us to ask not only who has power—and in particular whether the viewer of cute images is really the one with all the power—but also why we are so concerned altogether with power relations. "Why and to what end power?" is the question that, as I argued earlier, Cute poses; and no images do so more vividly than those of Yoshitomo Nara (see fig. 5.4).[11]

❖

The unpindownability of Cute as a way of being is the ideal expression of Japan's historical moment since 1945 and its will to purge itself of overt violence. But it also accords with potent, if stereotypical, features of national self-understanding: a genius for unclarity; for refusing definition; for skirting around all either/or; for being simultaneously in different and even contradictory places and moods; for allowing states of affairs to be both true and false; for being both naive and self-aware (and we are seldom sure with Cute where we are on that spectrum, either); for celebrating deformity in perfection or perfection in deformity—such as in the cultivation of wizened plants, the deliberately crooked shapes of the most prized ceramics, and, more generally, the aesthetic of *wabi-sabi*, or seeing beauty, even wisdom, in the imperfect; and pervading all this, an ineffable lightness of touch.

Many of these characteristics—which play such a prominent role in how Japanese and foreigners see the nation—are embodied in the haiku, "that mysterious seventeen-syllable utterance, in which a whole world is suggested by words that refrain from describing it":

yaa shibaraku
hana ni taishite
kane tsuku koto

Hey there, wait a moment
before you strike the temple bell
at the cherry blossoms. (Shigeyori, 1602–80)[12]

Or:

kyōnite mo
kyō natsukashi ya
hototogisu

even in Kyoto
longing for Kyoto
the cuckoo. (Matsuo Basho, 1644–1694)[13]

And so, Hello Kitty can show up with a face
blood-spattered by a "Gloomy Bear" with razor-
sharp claws, or as a World War Two kamikaze
pilot; but these violated or violent incarnations
don't seem to invite clear approval or disap-
proval. Pokémon's most popular monster, Pikachu, might be Japan's answer to Mickey Mouse,
but it is unmistakably Japanese in its freedom
from Manichean oppositions between good
and evil. And there is something Japanese, too,

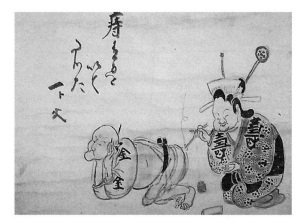

FIG. 5.5 Hakuin Ekaku (1685–1768), *Curing Hemorrhoids*, 56 × 64 cm. Eisei Bunko Museum, Tokyo.

in its wistful combination of gentleness and re-silience[14]—as we also find in the paintings and writings of Japanese monks as far back as the seventeenth century: for example, *Curing Hemorrhoids* by Hakuin Ekaku (1685–1768), one of the most revered masters of the Rinzai school of Zen Buddhism (see fig. 5.5).

This manifestation of the spirit of *kawaii*, such as we see in Hakuin's delicious sketch, with its freshness of touch, its ethereal playfulness, and its lighthearted sense of the grotesque, is also to be found, at about the same time, in the seventeenth century, in some *netsuke*: tiny carved ornaments that were "originally designed to serve an entirely practical purpose as toggles by which various items could be attached to the belt" around a man's robe, and so could be carried in the absence of pockets. Snails, pumpkins, hares, erotic figurines—the motifs of *netsuke* evolved over the next two hundred and more years with astonishing freedom and variety. They were often "humorous, grotesque and risqué"—in other words, remarkably cute, as we have characterized one of its moods here—in their "otherwise fairly naturalistic representation of deities, ordinary humans and animals."[15] (See fig. 5.6.)

Indeed, the sensibility that animates what is now called *kawaii* might stretch further back still than the sixteenth and seventeenth centuries. As long ago as the eleventh century, in the Heian period (794-1185 CE), seven

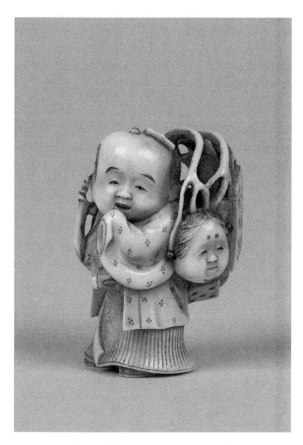

FIG. 5.6 Eighteenth-century ivory *netsuke*.
Metropolitan Museum of Art; Gift of Mrs. Russell
Sage, 1910; 10.211.484.

hundred years before the first recorded use of the word "cute" in the English language, and a thousand years before the contemporary cult of *kawaii*, the poetess Sei Shōnagon, courtier of the Empress Sadako, writes in a famous collection of her thoughts called *The Pillow Book* that "all small things are most adorable"; and she includes among such things:

> The face of a child drawn on a melon. A baby sparrow that comes hopping up when one imitates the squeak of a mouse. . . . A baby of two or so who is crawling rapidly along the ground. . . . A young Palace page, who, still quite small, walks by in ceremonial costume.[16]

Note that what Sei Shōnagon finds adorable is not just the face of a child: not just the sweet characteristics, such as those identified by Konrad Lorenz, that elicit protective responses in adults. It is, more whackily, the face of a child etched or drawn on a melon. A baby sparrow hopping towards one might be thought to be sweet enough; but what makes it more radically cute is that it responds to the call of—of all things—a squeaking mouse. Something unexpected, bizarre, exaggerated, distorted—this gives edge to what would otherwise be merely sweet. The same goes for the diminutive palace page in ceremonial uniform, rather than the page of usual height; or the *netsuke* depicting a snake curling around a pumpkin; or a toad sitting on a sandal; or the tiny, deformed bonsai tree.

What, in turn, is the origin of this predilection for the Sweet stretched or deformed into the more radically Cute? According to the renowned popular illustrator Miura Jun, the goofily cute characters that are found all over today's Japan and promote, as mascots, anything from regional specialties to local organizations to public events "are simply following the same ancient Shinto tradition that turned a myriad of gods, believed to reside in any animate or inanimate objects in nature, into 'characters' with specific names and personalities."[17]

This seems deeply right. The widespread human inclination to see spirits at work in nature and life—the inextinguishable animism that lurks in human nature, long repressed by monotheistic cultures but ultimately irrepressible—remains especially vital in Japan. Traditionally, many Japanese spirit-characters have a lighthearted, or even a cute, dimension: think of the rascally storm god Susa-no-o, who, in one of the founding myths of the Japanese nation, seeks to restore light to a world plunged into darkness by arranging for a comic spectacle to lure his sister, the sun goddess Amaterasu, out of the cave where she was hiding (and so depriving the world of light)—a spectacle that she just couldn't resist peeping out to watch.[18]

Or think of Murakami's *DOB in the Strange Forest*, which "finds Mr. DOB surrounded by staring, menacing plants and mushrooms"[19]—recalling the world of Shinto, where inanimate and nonhuman beings have spirits (see fig. 5.7).

FIG. 5.7 Takashi Murakami, *DOB in the Strange Forest (Blue DOB)* (1999). Fibre-reinforced plastic, resin, fibreglass, acrylic & iron. Private collection. Courtesy of Marianne Boesky Gallery, New York, © 1999 Takashi Murakami. Photo © Christie's Images / Bridgeman Images.

Or think, too, of the ancient cult of tree spirits (*Kodama*), cutified to an extreme in the film *Princess Mononoke*, Miyazaki Hayao's animated masterpiece (1997): a perfect example of the lighthearted, mildly alienating uncanniness of Cute, as distinct from the anxious and deeply alienating uncanniness

FIG. 5.8 *Kodama* (tree spirits) from *Princess Mononoke* (1997). Studio Ghibli. Photo 12 / Alamy Stock Photo.

that philosophers like Heidegger and Sartre describe; an emblematic instance of exactly that nimble, light-dark, goofy, androgynous unpindownability, that porous play between the familiar and the unfamiliar, which is the spirit of Cute (see fig. 5.8).

A woodcut of *Kodama* from around 1781 is no less cute in its very different style (see fig. 5.9).

Yet to connect the proliferation of spirit-characters in contemporary Japan to the rich history of Shinto deities isn't sufficient

FIG. 5.9 Toriyama Sekien, *Kodama* from the *Gazu Hyakki Yagyō* (c. 1781).

to account for the almost ubiquitous cutification of today's characters. The history might account for the impulse to populate the world with cartoonish figures, and it suggests that a sensibility of Cute has long been at work; but it cannot itself explain why such characters should, all of a sudden from the 1960s or 1970s, be so overwhelmingly imbued with cute characteristics, rather than with any other kind.

❖

To explain why today Cute, rather than any number of other sensibilities, has captured the Japanese imagination so comprehensively, and has come to animate an ancient tradition of character-spirits, we have to return to that central national mission of Japan after 1945: to repudiate the overt expression of power, nationally and internationally.

In so doing—in extirpating or sublimating the violent instincts, in forcing itself to be and appear peaceful—Japan is in the avant-garde of that wider international drive since the Second World War, extending to much of the West and to a degree still subterranean, in other words implicit and unspoken, to question and ultimately to escape the organization of life by means of power relations.

In the case of Japan, however, this tremendous national will to escape the power paradigm dovetails with a genius for indeterminacy, for the miniature, and for the playful to create today's protean culture of Cute.

Indeed, insofar as Cute is resolutely and light-heartedly indeterminate—insofar as it regards all resolution of unclarity as an impoverishment of spirit—Japan is its natural capital.

This is why it would, I suggest, be a mistake to see contemporary Japanese Cute as largely about girl culture and its devotees, including among men; or about the self-presentation of young women playing up to expectations of demure, vulnerable femininity; or about kinkiness or the fetishization of adolescent girls. These might be the original, most conspicuous, and still pervasive expressions of the postwar spirit of Cute, but they are only some of the forms that it can take. So, too, it seems wrong to interpret the Japanese obsession with Cute as motivated principally by a desire to flee from a regimented, hierarchical society, with its myriad calls to duty, into a cosseted state redolent of childhood—desire to flee seen, for example, in affected baby talk, or childish clothes, or the "fake child" that was a craze among many younger Japanese, under about age thirty, in the 1980s in particular. (In fact, it is key to the fake child, or *burikko*, and to its cuteness, that its child-like aspect is faked—and is *known* to be faked. To the extent that it is genuine, it is merely sad: an anxious hiding from the world.)[20]

Nor, I would guess, is cuteness a dominant language of intimate relationships in Japan. Although this is just my impression after a year living in the country and teaching at Tokyo University, deep intimacy in Japan—whether parental, sibling, romantic, or marital—seems remarkably *free* of the rituals and symbols of Cute. In romantic ties, the cute banter and horseplay that often pervade the gestures of early courtship appear to give way to a strikingly down-to-earth tone once a close and committed relationship has begun. Children, especially girls, might be showered with cute gifts by their parents; but the nursery and, in general, the family and its domesticity do not appear to be a primary site for the cult of Cute in today's Japan.

Instead, I suggest, Cute holds sway principally in *public* milieus, such as in young people's group personae; in the gestures of pop stars; in art, like that of Murakami and Nara; in the attempts of young professional women, as Sharon Kinsella puts it, to sugar-coat "their obtrusive new presence in the labor market by covering themselves in pink and candy and Hello Kitty, [so] disguising themselves as harmless" in a male-dominated work world that is widely "hostile" to their presence in it;[21] and, of course, pervasively in advertisements, consumer products, banks, police boxes, the armed forces, and government communications. According to Brian McVeigh, in corporations and other large organizations, it "reinforces vertical relations" of bosses to their subordinates, and especially of male superiors to their female inferiors, and at the same time "strengthens the notion that those in inferior relations require and need care and empathy from those in authority."[22]

Indeed, as we have seen, the psychologists Gary Sherman and Jonathan Haidt argue that, in general, Cute is best characterized as "a direct releaser of human sociality" beyond one's immediate offspring and family—and *not*, in the fashion of Lorenz, merely "as a direct releaser of caretaking behaviors" of a parental kind. Though the cuteness response might have originally evolved to ensure parental care and nurturing, it is, they claim, the perfect stimulus for motivating individuals to expand their circle of moral concern to an ever-wider social sphere.[23]

These findings of Sherman and Haidt dovetail with my suggestion that *kawaii* is most potent and prominent in social milieus, rather than in private spaces. If the cult of Cute in Japan is, as I have proposed, directly related to that great nation's will to convince itself and the world of its peaceful intentions, then the *public* realm is precisely where Cute must be most vital and creative. For it is here that the calamitous mistakes of the past were made; and it is here that *kawaii*, with its choreographed frivolousness, harmlessness, and indeterminacy, repudiates the cult of earnestness, brutality, and obedience associated with Japan's era of militarism.

6

The Cuteness of
Kim Jong-il

That Cute is about more than the Sweet—
that it also has a large hinterland of
indeterminacy—can be seen by asking oneself
a simple question: Which famous personalities are cute and which aren't? For example,
which political leaders?

We will each have our own list, but whatever our answer we will find that it comes to
us instantly and almost indubitably, and that
it in no way correlates to their goodness or
ethical probity, let alone to pure innocence,
helplessness, harmlessness, and other markers
of the Sweet. For me—though some readers

will disagree—Roosevelt and Churchill have an element of cuteness, whereas Margaret Thatcher and Charles de Gaulle do not. George W. Bush and Golda Meir do, but George Bush Sr. and Barack Obama do not. Bill Clinton does, Hillary Clinton doesn't.

Among the dictators, we can play the same game: for me, Kim Jong-il has a touch of cuteness—at any rate, for someone who was not under his rule (it would, of course, be absurd to speak on behalf of the North Korean people in this or in any other regard)—as does his father Kim Il-sung; but his son Kim Jong-un doesn't, for all his pudginess and soft contours.

Cuteness, I will suggest, is key to understanding Donald Trump.

One's intuition that a leader is cute isn't, therefore, founded in a perception that he or she is innately harmless, or innocent, or submissive, or good. The very different cases of Churchill and Stalin show that. Equally, an uncute leader—say, the much-lampooned former Japanese prime minister, Mori Yoshiro, or Britain's Theresa May—is not by that token vicious, strong, worldly, dominant, or evil.

So, too, a consideration of what each of us finds cute will quickly show that it isn't evoked just by vulnerable, small, infantile, cuddly, or sensuous features. Thus, for me, Charlie Chaplin is—perhaps surprisingly—not cute; but Sean Connery is. Lady Gaga isn't (and dressing up in Hello Kitty garb fails to change this); but Marilyn Monroe is. Madonna and President Xi of China are borderline.

This parlor game suggests some of the qualities that can be in undecidable tension when someone or something is cute. Not all of these pairs need be present, of course, to make it so:

- Strong and vulnerable
- Self-conscious and naive
- Venerable and absurd
- Conventional and zany
- Menacing and gentle
- Willful and diffident

- Limpid and mercurial
- Beautiful and gruesome

❖

And there is another expression of undecidability that often marks the cute, to which we have already alluded: namely, androgyny. The cute are seldom exclusively masculine or feminine, but rather possess features of both genders, as they are traditionally conceived, especially facial features. (We find echoes of this, again, in Japan: for example, in those young men who seek a more feminized masculinity by shaving bodily hair, plucking their eyebrows, and using cosmetics; in the male transvestism to be found in *butoh*, a form of contemporary dance, and in a celebrated group of portraits of eminent figures of the literary establishment, titled *Tamayura*.[1])

As we have seen, such figures as E.T., Hello Kitty, and *Balloon Dog* are strikingly androgynous. So are today's skinny models, male as well as female, with their spare torsos and gangly postures. And, in its own way, so too is Takashi Murakami's character Mr. DOB, whom we encountered earlier in "the strange forest" (fig. 5.7).

Like *Balloon Dog* or Mr. DOB, the cute political leader will frequently combine features of a male and a female face—but, again, in a manner that appears unresolved. For example, strength that is manifested as overt aggression, like vulnerability that is overtly weak, kills cuteness at once. People like Stalin and Kim Jong-il (unlike uncute tyrants such as Saddam Hussein or his merely vicious sons, Uday and Qusay) are careful not to be seen, or known, to kill people by their own hand. There is nothing, but nothing, cute about terrorist groups like the Islamic State or al-Qaeda.

It might therefore be no coincidence that Kim Il-sung was carefully portrayed as androgynous in North Korean poster art: "the hermaphroditic parent of a child race whose virtues he embodied"; not an unalloyed he-man, but a god of blurred gender. Indeed,

"Kim Il-sung's peculiarly androgynous or hermaphroditic image also seems to exert a far more emotional attraction than any of the unambiguously paternal leaders of [formerly communist] Eastern Europe were able to."[2] His willful, soft, clean images show him as both strong and morally pure, indomitable but never overbearing, combining the traditional virtues of a mother and a father in one person, and dedicated tirelessly, selflessly, and with divine composure to the well-being of his people, who are themselves soft and clean. Moreover, he is slightly plump, which symbolizes "the [Korean] race's newfound freedom to indulge its innocent instincts"[3] as well as, one presumes, their alleged prosperity, which he alone has bestowed upon them.

In short: a cute leader presiding over a cute people.

❖

It is key, though, that the behemoth with a touch of cuteness—Stalin, Kim Jong-il, Kim

Il-sung—isn't cute despite being a behemoth but because of it. Irresolvable indeterminacy, we have said, gives Cute its bite. Indeed, we find that the cute behemoth embodies an even more extreme form of ambivalence than androgyny—perhaps the most extreme of all possible forms: the ambivalence between the human and the nonhuman, or inhuman. He hints at the softness and roundness typical of the infant; but, like E.T., he also has something that appears entirely alien, something that makes him seem to inhabit not just the feelings of ordinary people but also a world that entirely transcends them, one that the common woman or man cannot reach or fully recognize.

Again, what is mesmerizing here is that the familiar becomes unfamiliar and the unfamiliar familiar. We become drawn to such a figure as into the interstices of a maze. His childlike features make his nonhuman nature—and its secret power—seem approachable at the same time as they throw into relief its utter strangeness. His monstrosity becomes all the more spellbinding because it's combined with ordinary human qualities. Like Hitchcock's birds, we are mesmerized by the horror of a creature that is also everyday. What we thought we knew suddenly becomes terrifyingly strange. Unfamiliar violence erupts from out of the most familiar of forms. We are unnerved by such neighborliness of the known and the unknown. And yet we are also excited by them because they give spice to the ordinary and access to the extraordinary (see fig. 6.1).

Kim Jong-il teaches us what it takes to have a touch of uncanny Cute (in other words, not to be at the purely sweet end of the cuteness spectrum). He, too, is androgynous—perhaps more so than his father. He appears childlike and yet is presented as all-knowing. He enjoys the superhuman safety of an absolute dictator, yet has a penumbra of vulnerability, being famously too scared to fly, seldom if ever appearing with a wife or family, and almost never speaking in public, as if afraid of being exposed at all.

FIG. 6.1 Official image of Kim Jong-il released on his death (2011) and carried aloft his hearse. Wikimedia Commons uploaded by Momocalbee.

To be this cute, striking unfamiliarity must abut homey familiarity. For clearly not all combinations of the human and the non-human are cute. The mermaid, for example, blends a young woman of generally clichéd beauty with the alien life of the fish—the warm-blooded creature with the cold—but isn't, on that account, particularly cute. Her unfamiliarity is too ordinary: too comprehensible. We know what a fish is; we know what a maid, as conventionally depicted, is.

The combination of the two knowns, each of them moderately drawn, does not leave enough of the sort of indeterminacy that can evoke the cuteness response.

Whereas Murakami's Mr. DOB, which *is* cute, conjures just that sort of indeterminacy. Painfully suppressed violence and vulnerability inhabit this quirky character, which, as we saw in figure 5.7, *DOB in the Strange Forest*, finds itself in a gently unnerving world of animated mushrooms and glaring plants, and which seems to combine both the early and the later Mickey Mouse, interweaving Mickey's originally menacing streak with his later put-upon mildness.

In a less intricate way, Jeff Koons's *Balloon Dog* also evokes a frisson of cuteness by presenting the familiar—the fragile demeanor of a little dog—in a conspicuously unfamiliar form: the monumentality of a sculpture made of high-chromium stainless steel—that most unsoft, unfurry, and uncanine of materials.

Some of the animals that seem to be regarded as cutest take us aback by doing something intensely human or otherwise alien to their species, like the penguin squeaking with glee as it's tickled, the puppy looking thoughtfully at itself in the mirror, the deer cuddling a cat.[4]

Thus the opposite or distinct attributes that, taken together, can most powerfully evoke the cuteness response are likely either to combine the familiar and the unfamiliar, such as a human and a god, or else to merge two seemingly familiar realms—such as the masculine and the feminine, the child and the adult, the animal and the human, the menacing and the gentle—in playfully incongruous ways that enhance, rather than resolve, the mystery of each.

Indeed, with such stubbornly indeterminate juxtapositions of the familiar and the unfamiliar, we touch once again on that fascinating phenomenon so integral to our experience of Cute in many of its forms. This is the phenomenon of the "uncanny," to which we now turn.

7

Cute and the Uncanny

In its most general sense, the uncanny isn't merely eerie or unnerving. It is an eeriness by which we are mesmerized.

We aren't drawn to a rustling noise in a dark alley that might signal the presence of an attacker. Nor to a distant roar that could be of a tsunami rushing towards our deck chair on the beach. But we might be riveted by a corpse that we are told could still be alive, or by a doll that bears a powerful relationship to a child we know, or by a creaking floorboard on which we can't see anyone treading, or by the coincidence of wishing something and then having it materialize before our eyes, or by the constant recurrence of the same number, say 48, in very different situations on a single day—the cloakroom ticket, the bus that has just arrived, the age of a friend whom we are told has died—or by noticing the same face looking at us each time we leave a building.

Why might we be drawn just to *this* sort of unnerving situation, rather than to any sort? Because, Sigmund Freud speculates, it revives infantile desires, fantasies, or archaic ways of thinking that were once known to us, or to our primitive ancestors, but have since been made unfamiliar or dismissed as mere superstition, because we have repressed them. The uncanny "is in reality nothing new or alien, but something which is familiar and old-established in the mind and which has become alienated from it only through the process of repression."[1] It is "that class of the frightening that leads us back to what is known of old and long familiar."[2]

But, we might continue to ask, why are we drawn to what we have repressed? We generally repress something that is unpleasant and that we want to forget about rather than return to. Why are we compelled to repeat our experience of it? Because, Freud claims, a compulsion to repeat belongs to the very nature of our instincts. Whatever reminds us of this unconscious compulsion to repeat is perceived by us as uncanny. And no instincts are more primitive and more reliably repeated than those underlying magical thinking and fear of the dead. We moderns imagine, he suggests, that we have surmounted archaic beliefs, such as those about the evil eye or ghosts and spirits; but they are merely repressed by us and can be quickly reactivated when they seem to be confirmed by unexpected events.

And here we return to cuteness, where we find a very particular expression of the uncanny: one that is playful, frivolous, muted. Koons's *Balloon Dog*, Kim Jong-il, and Hello Kitty's many manifestations all convey precisely such a sense of something that seems endearingly, even tenderly, familiar—yet also alien or monsterlike. Attraction to cuteness doesn't merely revolve around "the desire for an ever more intimate, ever more sensuous relation to objects already regarded as familiar and unthreatening."[3] Part of what makes Cute compelling is that in so many instances, it places side by side the strangely familiar and unfamiliar, which can seem to evoke each other, to oscillate between each other, without coming to rest in a settled relationship.

Thus, in each of these three cases, something familiar reappears to us as unfamiliar. The sort of dog that we have all known and wished to protect is re-presented as a vast dog that seems, spookily, to be both vulnerable and granite-hard; and this metamorphosis is not entirely unthreatening but, on the contrary, oddly threatening. The ubiquitous political leader is also a monster who is inaccessible and unknowable; the protector with the bouffant hair, who combines a hard stare and a soft smile, morphs into the superhuman arbiter of the life and death of his people; the father figure appears, on closer inspection, to be strangely androgynous. A sweet catlike girl is, by turns, a punk rocker or a pirate.

It hardly matters that cute objects can be so trivial. Indeed, that might be their whole point: for it is precisely when the trivial comes to seem unfamiliar that we are most struck by the uncanniness of the ordinary and so are able to experience it anew, as extraordinary.

❖

But an uncanny effect can also be generated by the reverse trajectory: what at first sight seems unfamiliar becomes streaked with the familiar. The grotesquely huge stainless steel dog also has something very ordinary about it. The remote political leader is imbued with soft, childlike features with which his people can readily identify. In each case, too, there is a hint of regression to an original condition: on inspection, the *Balloon Dog* comes to seem a very young dog; the adult dictator has a neotenous aspect; and in the case of

Mickey Mouse, regression to a juvenile state unfolds before the eyes of the world over a half-century.

And, crucially, the borders as well as the underlying connections between the familiar and the unfamiliar—and between the real and the fantastic, the rooted and the uprooted, the everyday and the extraordinary, the developed and its primitive precursor—cannot be located. Those border regions appear mysterious, and our attraction to the uncanny—as to the Cute—is driven, at least in part, by the charisma of that mystery.

For Freud, this mystery is a past, individual or collective, that has been repressed and that returns to us in unfamiliar forms: as ghosts, as the acts of dead ancestors, as magical occurrences, as doubles, as déjà vu, as coincidences too powerful to be accepted by us as mere chance. Moreover, he tells us, our pursuit of the mystery, and our surrender to the belief that what we had dismissed as superstition might after all be possible, carries great dangers: it can dissolve our selfhood and identity, knock our adult life and loves off course, and end up driving us to insanity.

We cannot penetrate the mystery, but nor can we avoid it. Like Cute, the uncanny eludes mastery at the same time as it invites it. Like Cute, the uncanny raises the question: Who has the power, the hunter or the hunted? Like Cute, the uncanny is unpindownable—indeed, it typically throws into doubt what we took to be familiar objects and categories. Like Cute, it might sow disorder and unclarity. Like Cute, it can seem to mutate between opposites, or to be both and yet in a full sense neither—thus blurring what are widely regarded as fundamental distinctions, such as between the human and the superhuman (Kim Jong-il), or the masculine and the feminine (Mr. DOB), or fragility and monstrosity (*Balloon Dog*). Like Cute, it is closer to our primitive self than we think that we, as adults, are or should be. And so it can make us feel a stranger to ourselves, trapped in a no-man's-land between our adult now and the child that we once were.

8

What's Wrong with Cute Anthropomorphism?

A frequent charge against Cute is that it is a narcissistic sensibility that imposes human qualities onto nonhuman things and so heedlessly anthropomorphizes the world. It cannot let anything it touches—nature, an animal, a piece of fruit—be in its Otherness. Instead, it is an imperialistic force that brings everything under human sway, compelling nonhuman things to fit into a human mold and to conform to human needs.

As we have seen, Daniel Harris, in his widely cited essay on cuteness, excoriates it for just this reason, damning "the cute world-view" as "one of massive human chauvinism." The rot starts early, according to Harris: "anthropomorphism is to a large extent *the* rhetorical strategy of children's books, which often generate their narratives from a kind of animal transvestism, in which dogs, cats, bears, and pigs" are forced into the "clothing and demeanor of human beings." It "creates a class of outcasts and mutations, a ready-made race of lovable inferiors whom both children and adults collect, patronize, and enslave." The "narcissism of cuteness" therefore means that "the cute vision of the natural world is a world without nature, one that annihilates 'otherness,' ruthlessly suppresses the non-human, and allows nothing, including our own children, to be separate and distinct from us."[1]

In a similar though more nuanced vein, Sianne Ngai sees "personification strategies" as "cuteness's master trope."[2] Such strategies easily become "a dominating gesture" that can end up maiming and silencing ("denying speech" to) its objects. Citing "The Orange" by Francis Ponge (1899–1988), a late modernist writer who composed a collection of prose poems on everyday things, such as an oyster or a cigarette, Ngai claims that this text exemplifies how endowing a dumb object with expressive capabilities can become just such an anthropomorphizing act of domination, indeed of injury. Ponge writes, in his Delphic fashion:

> Like the sponge, the orange aspires to regain face after enduring the ordeal of expression. But where the sponge always succeeds, the orange never does, for its cells have burst, its tissues are torn. While the rind alone is flabbily recovering its form, thanks to its resilience, an amber liquid has oozed out, accompanied, as we know, by sweet refreshment, sweet perfume—but also by the bitter

awareness of a premature expulsion of pips as well.[3]

For Ngai, the act of making the orange expressive, "in the sense of making it articulate and meaningful but also in the sense of forcing it to expel its 'essence,' is in effect to subject it to injury." She refers in particular to the line "its cells have burst, its tissues are torn." And so, far from being an empowering act, she sees it as "an act not just of humiliation but of mutilation."[4]

Ngai's analysis of the relations of power at work in Cute is subtle, and it allows for an imagined "revenge" on the part of cute objects against their perceiving subject, so that they can be experienced as "helpless and aggressive at the same time,"[5] controlled and, in their turn, taking control. Thus, she argues, a reversal is possible in that "if things can be personified, persons can [also] be made things."[6]

Yet for all the "oscillation between domination and passivity, or cruelty and tenderness" that Ngai detects in the aesthetic of cuteness, for all its "defining dialectic of power and powerlessness," which "seems to always include a fantasy of the agency of its hyper-objectified objects," Ngai appears to conclude that Cute's "master trope"—in other words, personification of its objects—ends up manipulating and exploiting those objects, despite (or because of?) ascribing agency to them.[7]

❖

But there is another way of looking at the anthropomorphizing effect of Cute—namely, to see Cute's power to personify its objects as precisely a way of recognizing and honoring their Otherness. Which is, perhaps, just what Emily Dickinson does in many of her severely cute poems. Pygmy seraphs, elfin mushrooms, and chubby-cheeked squirrels are some of the denizens of Dickinson's cute universe, in which, as Angela Sorby elucidates, she engages "not just with conventionally fluffy animals, but also with insects, graves, and corpses; with an endangered Protestant

God; and with questions of time, space, and scale."[8] Here, personification becomes a way of achieving empathy rather than injury.

In, for example, a letter to T. W. Higginson, grieving over the death of his baby daughter, Dickinson includes a short poem:

A Dimple in the Tomb
Makes that ferocious Room
A Home—[9]

At first, it might appear that evoking an infant's dimple—something of unquestionable cuteness—is a perfect example of how Cute domesticates and distorts its object, in this case by imposing the demeanor of the living on what is most inconceivably alien from human life: namely the domain of death. The image of a dimple is even said to make the "ferocious Room" of death—the tomb—into a "Home," thus imputing human life into what, by definition, completely lacks it. For death and home lie in diametrically opposite directions, as Odysseus laments to his men when the goddess Circe tells him he must visit Hades before he can return home to Ithaca:

> You think we are headed home, our own
>   dear land?
> Well, Circe sets us a rather different
>   course . . .
> down to the House of Death and the
>   awesome one, Persephone,
> there to consult the ghost of Tiresias, seer
>   of Thebes.[10]

And yet Dickinson's poem, in its magical brevity, does the very opposite of domesticating its object. To be sure, mention of the dimple immediately triggers those parental caregiving instincts described by Konrad Lorenz. We feel a moment of consolation—or if not consolation, of humanization of the darkness and decay of the grave. We imagine the plucky survivability of the cute infant who lies in it. We are inspired to hope that the grieving father might feel close to his lost child. But this fleeting consolation makes the letdown all the greater; for in disarming our resistance to the reality of death, it quickly brings us closer to that very reality. The rush of cuteness makes us all the clearer that the father can no longer protect, or even touch, his daughter. She is gone; the dimple is nothing but a fantasy imputed, in vain hope, to her corpse; the coffin is closed.

❖

Dickinson shows us how not only literature but also concepts can be cute in just the sense of remaining ineluctably playful, absurd, dark, and frequently concerned with an object that is small and vulnerable, yet retains undeniable power over us as subjects.

Here is another cute poem, about a dead mouse rather than a dead child. It pleads with God to grant the mouse an afterlife in snug seraphic cupboards:

Papa above!
Regard a Mouse

O'erpowered by the Cat!
Reserve within thy kingdom
A "Mansion" for the Rat!

Snug in seraphic Cupboards
To nibble all the day
While unsuspecting Cycles
Wheel solemnly away![11]

It is hard to see how the mouse is humiliated, mutilated, or injured by this poem's "personification strategy." On the contrary: Isn't Cute employed here to charm God into treating mice as he treats humans, and so into bestowing equality on all Creation? Moreover, doesn't the poem implicitly rebuke the divinely ordained dominion of humanity over the rest of the animals—the special status of human beings, to whom God gives the earth and its creatures as their fiefdom (Genesis 1:28–31)?

But, of course, we don't know whether God is really being rebuked. The verse is cute not only because it concerns a put-upon mouse or on account of its lighthearted tone, addressing God as "Papa above!" but also in its playful unclarity. An unclarity that, as it happens, finds echoes in Scripture itself. For Scripture is indeed ambiguous about whether the rest of Creation is necessarily less favored than humans. On the one hand, God gives humanity stewardship over the animals—albeit one that can and should be read as responsible care rather than as a license for selfish exploitation. (In the book of Genesis, humans are created to be vegetarians, quite reasonably, for on the whole, good rulers do not eat their subjects.)[12]

On the other hand, Scripture is strikingly protective of the animals. For example, many more animals than humans are saved on Noah's ark after God orders the flood that will destroy life on earth: "And of every living thing, of all flesh, you shall bring two of every kind into the ark, to keep them alive with you; they shall be male and female."[13] Thus all species of animal are to be rescued; but only one family of humans.

Elsewhere, in the book of Proverbs, we read that human beings are to learn from the animals—and even from the lowly ant.[14] And the book of Ecclesiastes, written, it is said, by the wise King Solomon, proclaims that "the fate of humans and the fate of animals is the same; as one dies, so dies the other. They all have the same breath, and humans have no advantage over the animals." And it adds: "Who knows whether the human spirit goes upward and the spirit of animals goes downward . . . ?"[15]

❖

Cute's power to recognize and honor Otherness is also identified in the work of the psychologists Gary Sherman and Jonathan Haidt, whom I cited in chapter 1. By motivating human sociality, they argue, "cute entities become objects of moral concern and members of the moral circle." Precisely *because* the cuteness response anthropomorphizes, it draws others into our moral circle, pulls strangers closer, and endows them with new value. In this respect, it is the real opposite of disgust, which "shrinks" the moral circle—refusing to extend intimacy or care or value to others, or even to look at them.[16] Thus, whereas disgust recoils from others, Cute reaches out to them. Whereas disgust dehumanizes, Cute humanizes.

Indeed, the more unlike us others are, the more we must impute to them human feelings and human characteristics—such as vulnerability, pain, and the need for protection—in order to unleash that sense of fellow feeling. Anthropomorphizing, to the extent that it extends our circle of concern, therefore makes possible such empathic access to the Other. In doing so, it can jump species barriers between humans and the rest of the animal world—and between the living and the inanimate.

Thus the cuteness response, as Sherman and Haidt characterize it, is remarkably broad in its reach, ranging beyond the childlike to beings of potentially any age; beyond the boundaries of one's own family, ethnicity, and nation; beyond the human to other animals, such as ducks and pandas; and beyond the animate to the inanimate: to cars, handwriting, chirpy sounds, poems, and many other things. Because so much, human and nonhuman, living and nonliving, can be experienced as cute, it can extend the scope of our sympathies—and of those whose well-being we care about—far and wide, precisely by seeing others as in crucial respects like ourselves, precisely by dissolving the sense that they are alien or strange.

But, we should add, not automatically.

On the one hand, humanizing others—seeing them as sharing key human possibilities and vulnerabilities, and even as a second self whose well-being is crucial to ours (like Aristotle's conception of "perfect friendship")—can open up a channel to them, through which we are able to glimpse and respond to what is really specific to their nature, their needs, and the conditions for their flourishing.

That humanizing others induces us to be humane towards them is why torturers and killers are routinely taught to see their victims as lacking all such commonality—and so as subhuman. Here, humanization really is a cardinal sin because it makes fellow feeling possible, for the torturer breaks down only when he sees his victim as human. (The ancients believed that the invulnerable, self-sufficient gods must be incapable of compassion precisely because those gods didn't share, even potentially, in human needs and vulnerabilities.)

On the other hand, humanization can also close down our vision of others by indeed treating them as vessels into which we narcissistically pour our own particular world—our perspectives, our values, our needs—accompanied by the implicit or explicit demand that they be like us or conform to what we can tolerate. It can foist our way of being onto them, so that in drawing them into our circle of concern, we attempt to tame, suppress, even obliterate who they are in themselves, coercing them into a mold that isn't theirs, or isn't conducive to their flourishing. At the limit, this colonization and exploitation of the Other, who is thus forced into a position of inferiority, can become perverted into the sadism so often noted by critics of Cute.[17]

And yet, there is a larger point that is easily lost amidst all these pros and cons. Beyond questions about whether cute objects are colonized or, by contrast, empowered by their perceivers; about whether they are in inferior or superior positions; about whether their Otherness is respected or violated; about whether they are given a voice or condemned to silence; about whether they are included in the circle of moral concern or shut out of it—beyond all these questions is the matter of whether we do justice to the essence of Cute by seeing the relationship between perceivers and cute objects, so conventionally, in terms of strategies of empowerment or disempowerment. And, more generally, whether we aren't impoverishing

our understanding of human intentions, relations, and values by framing them so dog-
gedly in terms of the power they seek or
manifest. Our kneejerk fixation on power to
explain and evaluate our relations to others is,
I suggested earlier, the culmination of a very
particular philosophical tradition that arises
in the seventeenth century with thinkers
such as Hobbes and Spinoza, and progresses
via Nietzsche, Foucault, and many others—
and has become almost unquestioned second
nature in our time. But does the power paradigm really capture more than one dimension
of our relations to others? Does it enable us
to explain and evaluate as much about those
relations as we tend to think it does?

Cute is one—perhaps very trivial, very
tentative—way of exploring whether and how
the paradigm of power can be exited. Indeed,
as exemplified by the explosion of *kawaii* in
Japan, this might be one reason why it has
stormed those parts of the world—notably
Europe, the United States, and Japan itself—
that since the Second World War have sought,

intermittently and with many setbacks, to reduce the role of power in determining the structure of human relations, and most conspicuously of international relations.

Cute is a harbinger of what the future might hold: namely an overcoming of a master trope that insists on understanding human life predominantly in terms of the exercise and projection of the subject's will to power. Such an overcoming seems paradoxical, for, conventionally seen, the craze for Cute is centrally about power: about vulnerable objects being lorded over by more powerful subjects; about the "aestheticization of powerlessness"—indeed, about "not just an aestheticization but an eroticization of powerlessness."[18] So that even when a cute object is seen as, so to speak, "fighting back"—when it and its perceiver are taken to be locked in a dialectic of power or a struggle for power, Cute is still understood in terms of the power relations between a subject and a cute object.

But what if Cute is a miniature Trojan horse in the citadel of power: in the intellectual citadel that for over three centuries has increasingly interpreted even the most altruistic, compassionate, freedom-giving human relations in terms of power and the will to power? What if its real "master trope" is not personification strategies understood as projections of power, whether for good or ill, but rather playful unpindownability: the carefree evocation of uncertainty as a fundamental characteristic of life and world?

9

Cute and the Monstrous: The Case of Donald Trump

Our discussion of how the cuteness of Kim Jong-il depends on the human and the super-human abutting each other in ways that enhance the mystery of each; of how Cute is uncanny because familiarity and unfamiliarity border, indeed, flow into each other in unsettling and often unresolvable ways; of how *kawaii* would be eviscerated of its power were it an empire of the merely Sweet—were there no sting of absurdity or indeterminacy to its harmlessness: all these point to another way of characterizing what makes Cute so compelling. This is the *monstrous*, that ancient archetype of which we can see the Cute as a very recent and specialized manifestation.[1]

Why specialized? Why isn't the monstrous (or, indeed, its near neighbor the grotesque) always cute? Because the monstrous is cute only when its strangeness—the imaginary or fantastic character that animates it— discomforts in a comforting way: in other words, when the bizarre distortions and juxtapositions of qualities that give it its monstrous character can be seen not only as destructive, aggressive, unreachable, and sinister but also as protective, tender, addressable, indeed charming and even playful.

But the fascination of the monstrous does not lie just in its contradictions: comforting/discomforting; accessible/inaccessible; comprehensible/incomprehensible; familiar/ alien; charming/menacing; comical/grim. It also lies, crucially, in the perception that those contradictions are irreconcilable— irreconcilable to the point where the monstrous being appears to be a hybrid of two or more radically distinct beings that, in their essential nature, have nothing to do with each other.

Such baffling hybridity is key to the monstrous, as it often is to the cute. We find it as far back as the prehistoric caves of Les Trois Frères in Ariège, France, where we see bears with the head of a wolf, or with the tail of a cow, or with the spotted fur of a leopard. We can recognize the elements separately, but what are we to make of the whole? How is the familiar behavior of each element—a wolf, a cow, a leopard—going to be expressed in the compound?

Depending on how we view such creatures, we can expect utterly different things from them. They are endlessly mysterious, and thus endlessly compelling. They have the aura of the sorcerer. They inhabit a realm of magic.

Indeed, in the same cave, we find just that: the sorcerer with human feet and legs, eyes like a cat's, a tail, the antlers of a deer, and long furred ears.[2] Onto these imaginary forms, our ancestors could project all manner of hopes and fears, powers to save and powers to destroy.

Here, too, belongs the sphinx of ancient Egypt, also a hybrid of human and animal and also notoriously mysterious in nature and intent. Appearing as a threat to some and as a source of salvation to others—an object of both fear and love—from the time of Middle Kingdom Egypt, sphinxes bear the features of "the ever-victorious pharaoh."[3]

❖

The sphinx with the head of the "ever-victorious pharaoh" is where Donald Trump comes in. He embodies such archetypal incompatibilities of the hybrid and the sorcerer. Like other instances of the monstrous, they cannot be resolved. What is a bear with the head of a wolf? What is a human with cat's eyes? What is the inner world of a sphinx "really"?

Similarly, who is Trump, the whole person? What do the combed-back, dyed-blond hair and the puckered, pouting mouth mean? What elements of his personality do those repetitive hand gestures, at once reassuring and ominous, beckoning and distancing, speak of? Does he believe his truths? Does he believe his lies? We do not know.

But there is a further point about Trump—as about the monstrous. It isn't just that these questions are unanswered or unanswerable, but also that it is crucial to Trump's spell, as it is to the monstrous archetype, that indeterminacy reigns. Thus to anyone under his spell, no answers are sought or needed. Like a carnival of the grotesque, he both summons an alienated world *and* offers relief from it—both conjures and at the same time subdues "the demonic aspects of the world."[4] He can evoke the sinister and the consoling, the malevolent and the benevolent, the destructive and the creative, the false and the true, the promise of chaos and the promise of order; and these "inconsistencies" draw power precisely from *not* being resolved.

Thus, nothing can be allowed to appear determinate more than fleetingly. If Trump just conjured chaos—if he just set about destroying all those national and international institutions that he sees as benefitting only his foes; if the turmoil of his administration were perceived by his supporters as merely anarchic, rather than as symptomatic of his mission to subvert a fossilized order—or, by contrast, if he just presented himself to them, in the manner of a conventional politician, as a savior who could create a reliable world comprising a secure society, economy, and identity—he would lose his magic. If he were consistently menacing or consistently reassuring, or if he found a stable equilibrium between the two, he would cease to compel. He is sustained, not undermined, by his contradictions. His hold over his base depends on them. He embodies them as performance art.

To the extent that he is, in this way, unpindownable, Trump has a touch of Cute. It is not of first importance to his spell, therefore, whether he genuinely believes what he says; whether his words and actions faithfully express his feelings or intentions: in other words, whether he is sincere. It doesn't even matter whether he merely *takes* himself to believe what he says. As we will see in chapter 13, Cute steps outside the realm of sincerity, not because it is overtly insincere, which it isn't, but rather because it has nothing to do with sincerity. Here, too, unlike other politicians, who think sincerity matters to their voters and who at least try to fake it, Trump wins out by being cute—something none of his rivals for the American presidency, whether Republican or Democrat, could be or dared to be.

❖

That Trump's fans delight in his unpindownability, in his protean mutability and inconsistency, in his power to inspire the demonic as well as to subdue it, does not entail that they aren't also frightened and even alarmed by him—just as devotees of the Gothic novel take pleasure in its strange horror, or just as John Ruskin views the power of the grotesque as residing in its juxtaposition of the fearful and the ludicrous: in the way it plays imaginatively with what is otherwise forbidden or inexpressible.[5] For in the grotesque, what is alarming and baffling can also be a source of safety and reassurance.

This is why Trump doesn't come across as cynically double-faced in what one might call the "straightforwardly devious" way of a machine politician. Rather he seems to be a genuine chimera and to have a genuinely hybrid nature, redolent of the monstrous archetype. As a result, we don't know precisely what to expect of such a creature. We can't be sure what he really represents or stands for. Or whether there is any bedrock there.

In these respects, Trump has a distinguished lineage. In a superb analysis of the grotesque in nineteenth-century fiction, Thierry Goater says of Thomas Hardy that it is no wonder he can baffle those who read him. For he "outrageously distorts reality and crudely combines genres and modes." He does so in order "to reveal and give form to the ever-changing . . . world, a world threatened by meaninglessness." His aim is to evoke "the fragmentation of the world and of the subject, the inhuman, the abject, madness and death," thus allowing his devotees "to experience chaos from a distance while sensing the threat involved" and, indirectly, to posit a different and new existence.[6]

In short, the formula of Donald Trump.

10

Cute and the New Cult of the Child

Interest in the cute is routinely deemed infantile—or infantilizing; indeed, excoriated as such. Judgments of this kind take for granted that the aesthetic of Cute is centrally about attraction to the innocence or powerlessness of the childlike, motivated not just by the instinct to protect but also, variously, by the desire to regress oneself to childhood, to escape the demands and complexities of adulthood, and to be unthreatened and in control. Escapist and trivial at best, narcissistic and sadistic at worst, such motivations, it is said, end up belittling both the viewer and the object viewed.

As we have seen, such themes are common to reflections on Cute, whether by a maker of cute artifacts like Takashi Murakami, who laments that it has "castrated" his own country; or a scholar of contemporary Japanese culture such as Sharon Kinsella, who sees the pervasiveness of *kawaii* as reflecting "fashionable infantilism"; or a historian such as Gary Cross, who sees it as a flight to "wondrous innocence"; or the essayist Daniel Harris, who also claims that Cute aestheticizes helplessness, derides it as an "antiquated religion of infantilism," and asserts that it "almost always involves an act of sadism."

But do infantilism, escapism, and sadism, along with the desire for intimacy with familiar objects and the instinct to protect our young, really exhaust the motives for attraction to Cute? I don't think they do. Charges of infantilism, especially when they get lost in a fog of moralistic outrage, miss other possible and powerful motives: above all, motives that derive from a revolution in the valuation of childhood and in the treatment of children that has been under way, at least in the Western world, since the middle to late nineteenth century—in other words (and perhaps not coincidentally?) since almost exactly the time that the age of Cute itself dawned.

It is a revolution of astounding speed and scope, in which the world of the child has become ever more present to the adult as the key to a flourishing life; as the repository of the sacred; and increasingly as the highest object of love—a revolution that has resulted in the child's safety and security becoming a litmus test of society's moral health to a degree that would have been inconceivable for most of Western history.

Thus in just a few decades, from around the 1850s to the 1930s, an era in which heavy manual child labor and unremarked sexual abuse were common gave way to a world where children would become the embodiment of supreme value—and their violation, exploitation, or desecration among society's greatest taboos. Over the same time, the rise of psychology and psychoanalysis promoted a picture of the child as parent to the adult, and childhood experience as ineluctably embedded and at work in almost every success, failure, fear, vulnerability, strength, love interest, and career choice of an individual's life. And later in the twentieth century, the child began to gradually displace the romantic partner as the archetypal object of love, and its psychological health became a preoccupation of perhaps unprecedented intensity and moral significance.[1]

In addition, has there not also been a Western trend of more recent origin, dating from the 1970s or 1980s, towards the erosion of previously accepted borders between childhood and adulthood—a trend of which the rise of Cute might be one expression, or to which it might speak? Are we not seeing, on the one hand, children behaving in ever more adult ways, in particular in terms of a sense of their autonomy as choosers, valuers, and consumers, but also in their clothes, speech, sexual awareness, and familiarity with the media, very much including social media; and, on the other hand, the self-conception of adults becoming ever more vividly governed by a conviction that childhood is *the* ongoing determinant of the whole of life, from adolescence to old age—and therefore that the child is always present and always active in the adult? There has certainly been no shortage of voices since the 1980s, if not earlier, lamenting the "disappearance of childhood," as Neil Postman does in a classic tract,[2] and picturing childhood as "threatened, invaded and 'polluted' by adult worlds."[3]

Whether or not we regard childhood as a social construct, rather than as a developmentally distinct stage of life that can be identified in all cultures and at all times; whether or not we accept the controversial claim, notably of the historian Philippe Ariès, that, in Europe, the very concept of childhood as a separate phase of life didn't exist until it was "discovered" in the sixteenth and seventeenth centuries;[4] whether or not we hold that childhood is a different world and culture, even "a different order of being" to adult life[5]—there seems to have been a great blurring of recently and widely accepted demarcations between child and adult.

It is a blurring of demarcations in which the child's experiences are increasingly (indeed, to an unprecedented degree) taken to structure the adult's world; and in which the adult's ethos of autonomy and of sexuality is increasingly seen as invading the domain of the child. Perhaps not surprisingly, it is echoed in a great many cute objects and their devotees. A figure like Hello Kitty is not consistently either adult or child (though she is described as a little girl); nor, as we have seen, are Kitty's fans exclusively one or the other. Works by artists such as Nara, Murakami, and Koons are similarly hard to assign. So, too, are E.T., who is both ten million years old and very childlike, and Japan's adolescent "Ambassadors of Cute."

If attitudes towards the nature and valuation of childhood, at least in Europe and North America, are changing in anything like these ways—on the one hand, making childhood ever more sacred and, on the other hand, eroding traditional boundaries between it and adulthood—then we might have identified another reason for the rise of Cute. Namely, that in its much-criticized emphasis on the "infantile," and in its intrinsic indeterminacy between the childlike and the mature, the blank face and the knowing face, the asexual and the sexual, the aesthetic of Cute might once again be remarkably attuned to the zeitgeist—a playful, often trivial, but accurate expression of the spirit of the times.

Childhood as Sacred

Since the rise of Cute from the mid-nineteenth century runs strikingly parallel to the revolution in the value and sacredness of the child over that time, let us look at the latter in a little more detail. It is a fascinating story.

Today we take it as self-evident that there can be no life more precious than that of a child and no form of exploitation, whether economic or sexual or emotional, more heinous than that of children. Yet it was only in the mid-nineteenth century that child labor came to be regarded as unacceptable in, for example, the United States—and then principally within the urban middle class. Indeed the economic exploitation of children from American working-class or agricultural families continued to *increase* through the nineteenth century.[6]

As Walter Trattner has shown, child labor wasn't abolished in the United States until the early twentieth century, before which "ten year old boys were commonly found in the blinding dust of coal breakers, picking slate with torn and bleeding fingers," while "thousands of children sweltered all night for a pittance in the glare of the white-hot furnaces of the glasshouses."[7] And it was as late as the 1930s, as Viviana Zelizer writes in her brilliant study of the valuation of children in

America, that, partly thanks to child labor laws and compulsory education, "lower-class children joined their middle-class counterparts in a new nonproductive world of childhood, a world in which the sanctity and emotional value of a child made child labor taboo."[8] Zelizer documents "the profound transformation in the economic and sentimental value of children—fourteen years of age or younger—between the 1870s and the 1930s," which saw children of all classes become "economically 'worthless' but emotionally 'priceless.'"[9] So that an era in which the newborn was commonly "welcomed as the arrival of a future laborer" gave way to a new sensibility that held that—as Felix Adler, first chairman of the US National Child Labor Committee, put it in 1905—to profit economically from children is to "touch profanely a sacred thing."[10]

The astonishing speed with which the life of a child became invested with sacred value didn't only have the consequence that child labor went from being widespread to being almost completely unacceptable (though not without intense struggles or indeed some striking exceptions, such as child actors). Another result was that couples who couldn't have children of their own were suddenly willing to pay huge sums to secure a baby on the black market. Whereas a nineteenth-century mother had to pay to get rid of her baby, by the 1930s aspiring adoptive parents were forking out $1,000 or more to buy one. Indeed, "the market price of an [adopted] economically useless child far surpassed the money value of a nineteenth century [economically] useful child."[11] And whereas older boys were in great demand in nineteenth-century foster homes, from the 1920s onwards "adoptive parents were only interested in (and willing to wait several years for) a blue-eyed baby or a cute two-year-old curly-haired girl."[12]

Over these same few decades, society's attitudes to the sentimental and moral value of children were transformed by almost every other measure. The death of a child became a tragedy that evoked ever more intense and overt mourning, indeed much more so than most adult deaths—and one that was caused by accident, malnutrition, or disease "became a visible and embarrassing anachronism to a society newly committed to the welfare of its children."[13] The health and safety of children became a major moral priority, for which the state took increasing responsibility (with startlingly rapid results: over just six years, between 1915 and 1921, infant mortality in the United States decreased by 24 percent).[14] Insuring a child's life went from being acceptable practice to being intensely controversial—and, to the extent that it was continued, premiums came to be calculated by reference to a child's sentimental value rather than its economic value. And, of course, child abuse, whether sexual or otherwise, became an extreme crime. Indeed, according to the distinguished pediatrician C. Henry Kempe, who created the concept of the "battered child," it is only our contemporary vision of the child, and perhaps especially the child's body, as the repository of the sacred that has made us so intensely sensitive to the matter of its desecration. A book on child abuse, Kempe and his wife Ruth claimed in 1978, simply couldn't have been written a hundred years previously:

> If an investigator from the 1970s were to be transported back to the nineteenth century so he could survey the family scene with modern eyes, child abuse would be clearly visible to him. In the past, however, it was largely invisible to families and their communities. Before it could be acknowledged as a social ill, changes had to occur in the sensibilities and outlook of our culture.[15]

❖

To the extent that we are witnessing a growing cult of the child—as sacred, as the archetypal object of love, and as the crucible of adult life—we will at once see Cute's preoccupation with the childlike in a very different light from that of the critics whom we cited in opening this chapter.

For instead of appearing predominantly as a flight from the challenges of adult life, or as manipulation of the innocent, Cute can also be understood as a way of evoking, thematizing, and prizing–in a lighthearted, unceremonious way–what has come to be taken as the most sacrosanct embodiment of the human.

Instead of standing merely for an "infantile" urge to regress to a protected world of childhood, we can open up another view of Cute as a celebration of childhood in all its complexity and newfound equality of status with adulthood. This is not an idealized view of a purely innocent childhood, but a view of childhood as being dark as well as light, ugly as well as beautiful, cruel as well as gentle, deformed as well as pristine. It is a view of childhood as both susceptible to evil–for many centuries expressed by the metaphor of inherited "original sin"–*and* as innately pure—paradigmatically represented by such Romantics as Rousseau and Wordsworth. As Wordsworth writes in his great ode to early childhood:

> . . . trailing clouds of glory do we come
> From God, who is our home:
> Heaven lies about us in our infancy![16]

And instead of insisting, as Harris does, that Cute is intrinsically disempowering, a "portable utopia" of innocence and guilelessness and other fetishized images that "we would *like* to see in children," Cute can be understood as dovetailing with a revolution, a century and more in the making, which, on the contrary, has given ever-increasing prestige to childhood and power to the child.

11

Survival
of the Cutest

The very different cute figures we have seen—
from E.T. to Mickey Mouse, from the endless
mutations of Hello Kitty to the deformed So
Shy Sherri—have another thing in common,
in addition to lightness and darkness, open-
heartedness and elusiveness, familiarity and
unfamiliarity, innocence and knowingness,
the human and the nonhuman, and all those
other dichotomies that we have considered:
they are valiant little survivors.

The vulnerability of the cute isn't there just
to be petted and protected, as it is with the
purely sweet. It isn't there just to flaunt its

powerlessness in relation to its perceiver—to the one who finds it cute. On the contrary, the vulnerability of the cute can also draw attention to their capacity for survival, in other words to their strength. Usually a strength all the more delicious for being discreet, delicate, surprising.

In other words, though the vulnerability that is intrinsic to so many cute objects might make their existence seem perilous, it can arouse far more than care or pity. In addition, and perhaps primarily, it points to their plucky, heroic persistence. Or, in the spirit of Cute, a playfully mock-heroic persistence.

Such objects are therefore cute not despite but because of their survival in the face of their vulnerability or misfortune. If they were to collapse, shrivel, and die, they wouldn't be cute at all.

And, crucially, they are cute because they seem to survive, mysteriously, out of their own resources—their own stamina, their delectable deviousness, their way of evading danger armed only with irony, innocence, and cunning. Whereas if the purely sweet survive, it is because they were protected, or just lucky.

As a result, instead of invoking vulnerability only in order to mock or exercise power over it, Cute also celebrates vulnerability, rescuing it from the margins of society or consciousness and placing it, protectively, in the mainstream.

Indeed we can go further: the cute are often seen not just as spirited survivors but also as protective of others. Far from Cute being centrally about an "aestheticization of powerlessness," and objects being "most cute when they seem sleepy, infirm, or disabled,"[1] the opposite can be the case. Then we, the perceivers of Cute, take *ourselves* to be the vulnerable ones, and we see the cute as coming to *our* rescue.

This reversal—in which the cute become protectors rather than, or as well as, the protected—might explain why so many fans, including adult fans, reportedly find Hello Kitty "mysteriously benign, even powerful."

According to the anthropologist Christine Yano, fans perceive Kitty as "loyal to them, seeing them through good times and bad times, helping them face crises, [and] brokering the challenges of daily life with her constancy." They experience Sanrio's catlike girl as consoling not only because she is a lovable object to care for, but equally, or more so, because they feel cared for by her. There is no evidence that they delight in her principally, or even partially, because her vulnerability offers them a sense of power over her, let alone of sadistic power. Rather, her fans actually "position *themselves* as powerless in the face of her charms,"[2] much as fans might do when worshipping a movie star or celebrity singer.

❖

Yet again, we see how cute objects and our relations to them scramble the hard-and-fast distinctions that we conventionally take to exist between the powerful and the powerless.

For now a character that lacks a mouth, and to that extent a voice, possesses the one form of power that most humans actually want to be exercised over them: the power to protect.

As we have seen, Mickey Mouse in his post-Second World War incarnation is another exemplar of this plucky capacity to persevere and, beyond that, to keep order in his realm. So, too, is the much more recent phenomenon of Kumamon, the official mascot of Kumamoto prefecture in southern Japan, in which kids and adults alike found consolation after Japan was hit by a 6.2 magnitude earthquake on April 14, 2016. For Kumamon was seen as a survivor, like the residents of the small town of Mashiki, whom he visited in a huge convention hall where hundreds out of the tens of thousands of people displaced from their destroyed homes were sleeping. He was their savior, their little comrade in adversity, still going strong after the earthquake despite his vulnerability and innocence. His visit to the convention hall of devastated Mashiki was "reported on TV and

FIG. 11.1 Japan's Emperor Akihito and Empress Michiko visiting Kumamon (2013). © 2013 Kyodo News.

in the papers as news, as if a long-sought survivor had stumbled out of the wreckage alive. The children, many of whom had lost their homes in the disaster, flocked around him, squealing, hugging, taking pictures. Their friend had returned."[3] (See fig. 11.1.)

This power of cute figures to protect and soothe, from Mickey Mouse to Kumamon, is surely only one instance of a larger phenomenon: namely, the power of animals, and perhaps *especially small animals lacking physical strength*, to offer comfort and consolation.

Millions of people—young or old, healthy or dying, living in families or on their own—find solace in pets, whether real or fictional.

And this power of the powerless to console in turn points us to a related phenomenon, one that is much older than Cute: namely the mascot. For many mascots embody the paradox that it is precisely in gentleness that we often find strength, precisely in the gawky or the clumsy that we perceive a quiet, undramatic healing power.

So much so that an institution that exists for the single purpose of accumulating and projecting power—namely the military—often adopts as its mascots the cutest creatures, rather than paragons of brute force. Thus the US Army's mascot is not a lion or a charging gazelle but . . . a mule. The world's most powerful navy finds strength in a creature of the gentlest resilience: the goat. By the same token, Britain's national icon, not least during the dark hours of the Second World War, was, for long, a bulldog: small, compact, plucky, gentle, determined. Fierce, but hardly a titan.

12

Cute and Kitsch: Identical Twins?

Have we, in fact, been talking in this book about Kitsch? Aren't Koons's *Balloon Dog*, Murakami's Mr. DOB, the Japanese figures Kumamon and Doraemon, and Hello Kitty all paragons of Kitsch? And so isn't Cute just another word for Kitsch?

The answer to these questions is no. We don't necessarily see cuteness in Kitsch—for example, in flowery wallpaper; in fake Louis XV furniture with exaggerated ornamentation; in dramatic images of power, achievement, and happiness deployed by totalitarian regimes; or in a porcelain Santa (see fig. 12.1).

FIG. 12.1 Porcelain Santa Claus figurine. F1online digitale Bildagentur GmbH / Alamy Stock Photo.

Intuitively there seems to be a distinction between these neighboring concepts. Kitsch is everywhere, but does it inspire the obsessive dedication aroused today by Cute? Kitsch "welcomes you to the restaurant, greets you in the bank, and smiles at you from advertising billboards, as well as from the walls of your dentist's waiting room";[1] but is it (any longer) as powerfully attuned to the zeitgeist? Why does Cute spawn a multibillion-dollar industry, but Kitsch—though it is big business and though, a priori, we might expect it to be at least as ripe for mass marketing as the cute—is far less commercially successful?

Before addressing these questions, it is worth noting that Kitsch has been lambasted in remarkably similar terms to those deployed against Cute. Kitsch, too, has been condemned not just for displaying bad aesthetic taste but also for being morally corrupt and corrupting. "The producer of kitsch," writes Hermann Broch, the early-twentieth-century Austrian writer, "should be judged as an ethically base being, a malefactor who profoundly desires evil."[2] Seeing high art as under intense threat from the mass-market forgeries of Kitsch, Broch goes on to compare it to the Anti-Christ, whose whole purpose is to imitate the real Christ so as to displace and destroy him: "The Anti-Christ looks like Christ, acts and speaks like Christ, but is all the same Lucifer."[3] The critic Clement Greenberg complains, in 1939, that Kitsch "is mechanical and operates by formulas," involving "vicarious experience and faked sensations . . . the epitome of all that is spurious in the life of our times."[4] Kitsch, remarks Karsten Harries more recently, "has always been considered immoral."[5]

This critical tradition is encapsulated by the Oxford English Dictionary, when it describes Kitsch as "characterized by worthless pretentiousness."[6] Which is the nub of the case against it: that it is counterfeit, whether it takes the form of cheap trinkets, such as souvenir knockoffs of the leaning tower of Pisa, or whether it has pretentions to be deeper, such as the fake Louis XV furniture that I mentioned at the beginning of this chapter or the garish propaganda images churned out by totalitarian regimes (see fig. 12.2).[7]

The philosopher Robert Solomon distills six main ways in which Kitsch, like sentimentality, has been found wanting: it provokes immature emotions; it manipulates our emotions; it evokes false (or faked) feelings; it expresses easy or superficial emotions; it is self-indulgent; and it gives us a distortedly benign vision of the world.[8] In short: artificiality; bad morals and bad taste; cheapness

FIG. 12.2 Nina Vatolina, *Thanks to Beloved Stalin for Our Happy Childhood!* (1950). Heritage Image Partnership Ltd / Alamy Stock Photo.

of emotion; lowbrow, gaudy aesthetics; and naive optimism: these are widely seen as both cause and effect of Kitsch.

Much of this charge sheet can be, and has been, leveled at Cute. It, too, can evoke immature, superficial, self-indulgent, homey, and otherwise sentimental feeling. And in such ways, Cute can indeed be Kitsch.

But there the parallels end.

Whereas Cute can be uncanny, straddling the porous border between familiarity and unfamiliarity, between the normal and the grotesque, Kitsch seldom is.

Whereas Cute, in the hands of a Murakami or a Nara, can be (or at least can appear) radical, inventive, or shocking, Kitsch is conventional—often defiantly and nostalgically so.

Whereas Cute toys playfully with relations or disparities of power between the viewer and the object, Kitsch doesn't.

Whereas Cute can, therefore, evoke both gentle and unsettling emotions, Kitsch tends, or at least strives, to evoke only the comforting ones—evicting everything painful, disquieting, or dismaying from its realm.

Whereas Cute is unpindownable (and the more so as it moves away from the sweet end of the spectrum), Kitsch is clear and transparent, quoting undeviatingly from the vocabulary of the known, recycling easily assimilated tropes, and consoling precisely because of this conformism.

Whereas cute objects, with their intrinsic vulnerability, evoke a struggle to survive—and, like Camp, a marginal, endangered existence, even, as we have seen, when they are experienced as protective—Kitsch seeks to conjure a world that is only safe, solid, and uplifting. And to that extent, Kitsch portrays a fake world and Cute a truer one.

Whereas Cute is perhaps the least self-conscious of the minor aesthetic categories (categories, also including Camp and Zany, that are conventionally, though now decreasingly, distinguished from "high art" or "avant-garde"; for as Arthur Danto puts it, "nothing outward need distinguish a work of art from the most ordinary of objects or events"[9]). Kitsch is among the most self-conscious.

The novelist Milan Kundera beautifully evokes the timbre of this self-consciousness. Kitsch, he writes, "causes two tears to flow in quick succession. The first tear says: How nice to see children running on the grass! The second tear says: How nice to be moved, together with all mankind, by children running on the grass! It is the second tear that makes kitsch kitsch."[10]

And a related point: whereas it is often the aim of Kitsch to either emulate or scorn the taste of those taken to be at the top of the social pyramid, such aspiration to status, such self-exaltation, is no part of Cute. Nor does Cute express any intent to imitate or displace high culture more generally. It seems neither socially nor aesthetically ambitious. It lacks the clear will to power that Kitsch can evince.

Indeed, whereas much Kitsch exists—it self-consciously stands—in *relation* to such ruling cultural and aesthetic standards, whether it mimics or opposes them, Cute's very existence is not parasitic in any comparable way on a wider world of taste. Thus Kitsch aspires to be an insider, but insofar as Cute is vulnerable and indeterminate it relishes being the outsider.

Finally, whereas Cute can ironize or even mock itself—a cartoon figure like Hello Kitty doesn't present itself as being *really* about a little British girl, as saying anything definitive about its subject matter—Kitsch tends to be in earnest. The last thing Kitsch accepts is that it is counterfeit, a simulacrum. It doesn't have doubts about itself. Gaudi's buildings in Barcelona might have elements of Kitsch or, as Susan Sontag claims, of Camp; but they are surely not cute. They cannot be cute because they are too ambitious, too vaultingly single-minded in their claims. For, as Sontag remarks, "they reveal—most notably in the Cathedral of the Sagrada Familia—the ambition on the part of one man to do what it takes a generation, a whole culture to accomplish."[11]

(Similarly Mae West might evince Camp or even Kitsch, but she is too earnest, even in her humor, to be cute; whereas Cary Grant can be.)

The upshot is that Cute, except again when it approaches the Sweet, might leave us in limbo, whereas Kitsch always returns us to familiarity. As the philosopher Tomas Kulka says, Kitsch, being "ultra-conservative," tends "to reassure us in our basic sentiments and beliefs, not to disturb or question them." Thus, he adds, "there shouldn't be anything disturbing or threatening in kitsch."[12] Where Cute can be uncanny, indeterminate, void of a center of gravity, and indifferent to our prevailing morality (in particular, as I will argue in the next chapter, to our cult of sincerity), it belongs to the nature of Kitsch to avoid precisely these unsettling dispositions—thus giving us, as Robert Solomon summarizes the charge, "a fraudulent, overly 'sweet' and benign vision" of life that "somehow 'blocks' our larger, nastier knowledge of the world."[13]

Milan Kundera makes the same point more pithily. Kitsch, he says, is an aesthetic ideal "in which shit is denied and everyone acts as though it did not exist."[14]

As Nara's children, So Shy Sherri, and other wordless, wounded confections attest, that, at least, cannot be said of Cute.

13

Exiting the Cult of Sincerity

Why can we speak of an "Empire of Cute" whereas it would sound absurd to talk of an "Empire of Sweet"? Why does Cute have bite, but Sweet seems insipid?

We have already pointed to an answer: Cute compels because—when it isn't purely sweet—it playfully expresses the indeterminacy that our age sees as characterizing all existence. In doing so it sidesteps ancient dichotomies, such as those between good and bad, masculine and feminine, adult and child, and human and nonhuman.

In the same vein, there is another way, at least in Europe and America, in which Cute is attuned to the temper of our times. It is one of the great antidotes to that cult which, since the late eighteenth century, has increasingly come to tyrannize the Western world and mire it in hypocrisy—though its ostensible purpose is precisely to wage war on hypocrisy. This is the cult of sincerity, inaugurated by Jean-Jacques Rousseau, for whom accurate self-disclosure, honest transparency of one's authentic self, is the supreme virtue. It is a virtue that is widely seen as truthfully revealing, to oneself and to others, one's inner drives, needs, and taste—indeed one's entire character—yet as submerged and inactivated by the pretenses demanded by society and by people's frantic quest for the approval of others.

Sincerity, too, depends on faith in an ancient dichotomy: this time between inside and outside; an inner world that is honestly and transparently manifested in outer expression. Matthew Arnold gives eloquent voice to this dichotomy—as well as to the elusiveness of such honest expression, indeed, to the difficulty of knowing whether we have attained it at all:

> Below the surface-stream, shallow and
>   light,
> Of what we *say* we feel—below the stream,
> As light, of what we *think* we feel—there
>   flows
> With noiseless current strong, obscure
>   and deep,
> The central stream of what we feel indeed.[1]

It can be no coincidence that Rousseau's longest philosophical work is his autobiography, unsurprisingly called *Confessions* (thus trumpeting its sincerity even in its title), in which honest self-revelation is praised again and again as the supreme good. "I desire," Rousseau proclaims there, "to set before my fellows the likeness of a man in all the truth of nature, and that man [is] myself." And he continues: "Myself alone! I *know* the feelings of my heart. . . . I have *shown* myself as I was. . . . I have *unveiled* my inmost self. . . ."[2]

"What you see is what you get" is the refrain that sums up this pretense to express exactly who one is and to be exactly what one expresses. The cult of sincerity demands that, as a matter of course, we make extravagant claims to know ourselves (one claims to know exactly what drives one), to show ourselves (one is able to express just what one feels, reliably and transparently), and to be authentic selves (what one says and does and feels expresses who one *really* is).

That genius of skepticism, the philosopher David Hume, was quick to point out Rousseau's deluded claims to speak faithfully of himself when he said of him: "I believe that he intends seriously to draw his own picture in its true colours; but I believe at the same time that nobody knows himself less."[3]

Today's explosion of memoirs and of public soul-baring, not least on social media; the sense that our life only feels truly real to us and to others once we have encoded it in autobiography, along with the inner states and values guiding it; the way in which human beings' age-old search for attention, recognition, and approval is now conducted through publicly parading one's tastes and feelings, one's likes and dislikes, and other details of one's life, presented to the world as accurate even if acknowledged to be transient—all this owes an indelible debt to Rousseau and his pioneering *Confessions*.

But, in fact, we can seldom be sure what drives our wants and needs—or that what we think we feel is what we really feel; or that what we say and do accurately reflects what we feel; or that our feelings, words, and actions express our authentic self, if there is such a thing.

An obvious example of this is love. Almost everyone who passionately avows love is sure of their sincerity, in that they genuinely take themselves to be expressing their inner feelings. But we know how often the tests of time show otherwise: how often these feelings fizzle out, readily fix on another person, end in acrimony, issue in unhappy or short-lived relationships, and turn out to be other forms of attachment or to be motivated by a loveless need for power, recognition, reassurance, and concealment.

What is true of the course of love is true as well of many, if not most, of our other emotions. As a result, much of our sincerity—and of the straightforwardness and transparency that we seek to project through it—ends up being faked. And the pressure to be sincere is a fertile source of sham and hypocrisy.

One consequence of such faking is dangerously to confuse our relations to each other with false expectations of our openness and accessibility—including glib promises of being true to others as if this were the simplest, rather than the hardest, of achievements. Shakespeare's Polonius famously articulates such glibness:

This above all: to thine own self be true
And it doth follow, as the night the day,

Thou canst not then be false to any man.
(*Hamlet*, Act 1, scene 3)

The fraud fostered by the cult of sincerity also ends up confusing our own identity: for if we refuse to see that who we "genuinely" are is, to a great extent, opaque, and that our words and actions cannot be assumed to express more than fragments or moments of our being—rather than a consistent, coherent, and transparent self—then we are living our life on the basis of a false self-image. Succumbing to social pressure to appear true and transparent to ourselves, we end up merely *playing* the part of the open, comprehensible, and self-knowing citizen or partner—fabricating the "honest Joe" persona demanded by the cult of sincerity. Nor even, by the same token, can we be said sincerely to play-act our sincerity.[4] The result, in other words, is to create a false self to which we claim to be true—a self that we present to others, and *especially* to those closest to us.

❖

Cute as a sensibility sidesteps this charade. Not by championing opposite values: not by making a point of being insincere—of saying and doing things that aren't really felt. Or of misrepresenting inner states. If it were to do so, if Cute merely waged war on sincerity, it would be charmlessly purposeful.

Rather, cuteness has nothing to do with showing "inwardness," whether that inwardness is conceived as stable or as changing. Instead, its power depends on irresolvable ambivalences that, as we have seen, shift unstably between familiar and unfamiliar, vulnerable and resilient, powerless and powerful, innocent and experienced, masculine and feminine, young and old. Moreover, the cute are often mute—in the case of Hello Kitty and Kumamon by being quite explicitly mouthless. So that even when they are garish and eerie, like some of Murakami's creations or one of Nara's seemingly violated children, they are terminally opaque: you can't make out an emotional "core," or what exactly they might be saying.

If the cute speak any language at all, it is the language of unpindownability. (Here they bear more than passing resemblance to the zany, who also can't be pinned down.) They aren't interested in parading their truthfulness—indeed, it hardly makes any sense to say that they are truthful; yet they don't necessarily lie. They can be intensely expressive; yet you aren't sure what is masked or where they really stand. They are harmless and comforting; yet, unlike Kitsch, in an edgy, discomfiting way. They are melancholic, but lightheartedly so. They toy with appearing infantile; yet they are too savvy to be purely infantile.

Moreover, they play with their unpindownability, magnifying it by fostering confusion about how much of it is genuine and how much is faked. They teasingly invite you to try to seize them. In doing so, they can seem to parade their vulnerability. They tempt the viewer to objectify them—and for doing so, they are, as we have seen, routinely excoriated by their critics. Instead of hiding their wounds, they transform them into charm.

All this can be frisky or it can be serious— or, as in the best cuteness, something indeterminately in between. What looks like masochism on the part of the cute can be just a way of pretending to be powerless, or of playfully parading powerlessness. And what they provoke is, *pace* Harris, less likely to be sadism, the humorless lust to hurt and humiliate, than teasingly rambunctious affection, or even just the sort of hug where we squeeze someone a little more forcefully than normal—as when we want to make a point about having missed them, or to reprimand them for having eluded us.

But, again, the cute mire us in uncertainty: Who is really exercising the power? And— also again—to what end the power? Even if they are weaker, more passive, more muted than their admirers, so what? Do we overrate equality of power in our relations with each other? What would a world look like in which all inequalities of power had been redressed? Could a world exist in which we go beyond redressing inequalities of power and somehow free human relations, or certain human relations, of determination by power—a world in which power no longer dominates, or is taken to dominate, our interactions with each other? As, for example, it doesn't in the finest friendships.

Cute's absurdity, its seeming lack of clear aims, its indifference to means-ends rationality (it might serve or achieve goals in the end, but not by formulating and pursuing them systematically), its delight in—apparently—not being in control and even in being put upon, its antithesis to the serious world of work and career and achievement, its implicit mockery of the received wisdom that the best relationships are those of "respect and openness among equals," and its enjoyment, on the contrary, of an unstrategic, irreverent, scrawny existence—all this makes it a break from the dominant ethic of our times.

This is an ethic relentlessly focused on clarity of purpose, clarity of expression, saying what we mean, meaning what we say, being in maximum charge of our life (our terror of vulnerability is often masked by the lip service we pay to it), preserving our security, ensuring, or at least pretending, that all our key relationships are founded on equality of power and respect, exploiting our abilities to the full, playing alive at all costs.

From the point of view of this prevailing ethic, Cute cannot, of course, be taken seriously. It is ridiculous and, in many ways, contemptible. It is chaotic, pointless, squandering, reactive, and frivolous, much like the "superfluous man" of nineteenth-century Russian literature—except in a contemporary register of devotion to the miniature and the ephemeral rather than the grand and the eternal, to the mass-produced pop-cultural everyday commodity rather than the elevated ideal. It seems pretty poor at squeezing the most out of life, appearing empowered, and knowing what it wants. It is terrible at fixing goals, specifying the "X steps" to attain them, and then going after them with blazing determination. And yet, in a society chained to that ethic, it runs riot.

14

"Lifetime Is a Child at Play"

If Cute were, however, *nothing but* aimless, reactive, and trivial, it would scarcely be as compelling as it is. Nor, like the art of Murakami, could it be so readily associated with glamour and cool, which are centrally about appearing sovereign, unreachable, and immune to manipulation or deformation by observers.

Cute seduces because it is also in the temper of our times to affirm, and even to delight in, the idea that uncertainty or indeterminacy is intrinsic to human life—for example, to knowledge, meaning, and ethics—at the same time as we *also* demand lawlike predictability, certainty, transparency, and clarity from each other and from the world. The Heisenberg uncertainty principle speaks so deeply to—and of—our epoch precisely because it postulates that ineliminable vagueness is intrinsic to a lawlike universe; that there is a fundamental limit to what can be known about the world. So that we cannot determine precisely and simultaneously both the momentum and the position of a quantum particle: the more perfectly we know one, the less we know the other.

Limits to knowledge, a lack of unshakable foundations for our understanding and values and decisions, open-endedness, indeterminacy, freedom from single master purposes: these are deeply attractive to the contemporary Western world. (Which is one reason, I suggested in chapter 5, why Japanese culture, with its affirmation, even celebration, of unclarity and uncertainty, has such a hold over the West.)

And, crucially, it also belongs to the temper of the times to affirm uncertainty in a manner that isn't solemn. Our warring souls—one rejoicing in open-endedness and indeterminacy and chance; and the other craving ever-greater safety and clarity and control—comprise a new, contemporary dualism of the Western spirit, which is no longer as riven as it was by the traditional dualisms of human and animal, or body and soul, or the mental and the physical, or the divine and the earthly, or the permanent and the transient—dualisms that have lost much of their hold on us.

Such lighthearted affirmation of uncertainty, such playful unpindownability, such freedom from ultimate goals and ends, such valuation of chance and the ephemeral, such a stepping aside from the cult of sincerity with its self-conscious striving after accurate expression of an "inner" world—all this is of a piece with a celebration of natural innocence that, in diverse ways, has gradually taken hold in the Western world since the late eighteenth century, since such figures as Rousseau and Wordsworth.

It is a celebration given paradigmatic form in Nietzsche's striving to restore "the innocence of becoming"—*die Unschuld des Werdens*.[1] For Nietzsche, the highest type of human being, the culmination of a long development, is the child, who knows nothing of duties and ends and means and guilt. The child "is innocence and forgetting, a new beginning, a game, a self-propelled wheel, a first movement, a sacred 'Yes.'"[2] In a note, he even likens God to the child at play: "'Play,' the useless—as the ideal of him who is overfull of strength, as 'childlike,' the 'childlikeness' of God, *pais paizon* [a child playing]."[3] And later in his life, he adds: "A man's maturity—consists in having found again the seriousness one had as a child, at play."[4]

Here Nietzsche, like many thinkers in the nineteenth and twentieth centuries, looks back to that ancient Greek sage, Heraclitus, who left only fragments of philosophy and who enigmatically but pregnantly said of the *aion*, variously translated from the Greek as "lifetime" or "eternity" or "time":

> Lifetime is a child at play, moving pieces in a game. Kingship belongs to the child.[5]

Though many, perhaps most, actual cute things and styles can be trivial, derivative, and repetitive, the spirit animating them—the spirit of Cute—is anything but. For it is one symptom of modernity's attraction to the innocence of becoming: modernity's attraction to understanding human life, indeed existence more broadly, as fundamentally ephemeral, aimless, blameless, without final ends or first causes or ultimate unities—and, moreover, as distorted and denatured by attempting to see in life or existence a "moral world order"; or to judge it as, all things considered, good or bad; or to seize it with one commanding vision. And such an understanding of life and existence, as exemplified in the spirit of Cute, is not in any way resigned or grim or complacent or tragic but is rather playful, unstable, partial, and often frivolous.

We deeply misunderstand Cute as a sensibility when we see it as merely an infantilizing aesthetic of powerlessness. And we misunderstand it still further when we take it to be centrally about a narcissistic desire to control, exploit, or violate familiar and unthreatening objects. For even if it is any of that—and for some devotees of Cute it can be, of course—it speaks of so much more. Its fleeting, floating forms lightheartedly celebrate the intuition that the ordinary, no matter how familiar or insignificant, is stubbornly uncanny; and that, for all our struggles to be securely at home in the world, we are misfits living in uncertainty. In giving style to our misfittedness and lightness to our uncertainty, Cute is able to inspire a sense of freedom—above all, freedom from the tyranny of identity and power: from a human life rigidly understood in terms of clear identities and degrees of power to which it strives to give sincere and authentic expression. For, as we have seen, cute things or people are often, perhaps usually, of indeterminate power, gender, age, ethnicity, and morality. And except when the relationship between the cute object and its admirer is perverted into the grimly sadomasochistic, Cute readily mocks power—indeed, places in question the very purpose and value of power as well as the matter of who is really exercising it.

Insofar as Cute speaks, in these respects, of the spirit of our times—of our age's experiments with, and groping for, such new ways of being—it is a realm of frivolity to which we should, perhaps, attend in all seriousness.

Acknowledgments

I am deeply grateful to Sarah Caro, my magnificent editor, whose enthusiasm for a book on this maverick topic (at least for a philosopher) and whose sensitive intelligence and guidance have been such an inspiration. It was a privilege and unalloyed pleasure to work with her, as well as with Hannah Paul, associate editor, whom I thank for her sage advice, for her superb support, and for kindly securing permissions to reproduce the illustrations.

I also thank Terri O'Prey, my great production editor, who saw the manuscript through to publication; Molan Goldstein, from whose painstaking copyediting and thoughtful recommendations I richly benefitted; Theresa Liu, who honed the sales copy; Kimberley Williams, who managed the production of the audio book; Caroline Priday and Julia Haav, who oversaw publicity; Steven Moore, who compiled the index; Pamela Schnitter, book designer; Jacqueline Poirier, production manager; Amanda Weiss, who designed the cover; Stephanie Rojas, marketing and social media associate; Charlie Allen, editorial assistant; and all the others at Princeton University Press for whose skill and dedication I am grateful.

I am greatly indebted to Jeffrey Alexander, Stephen Bayley, Stéphane Beaujean, Simon Blackburn, Joshua Dale, Jessica Frazier, Sacha Golob, Andrew Huddleston, Robert Jackson, Sharon Kinsella, Griseldis Kirsch, and Stephen Macedo for their very valuable comments on the text.

My wonderful research assistant, Sarah Pawlett-Jackson, checked the notes, references, and bibliography with her unrelenting attention to detail, and made many important suggestions. As ever, I cannot thank her enough for her meticulous work.

Warm thanks are due to my agent in New York, Peter Bernstein.

This book is dedicated to Mimi Durand Kurihara, who inspired it in almost every way.

Notes

Preface

1. I use "Cute" as a noun to refer, variously, to cuteness as a property of objects and/or to the subjective cuteness response, in an analogous way to Susan Sontag's use of "Camp" as a noun—which she also capitalizes—in her iconic essay "Notes on 'Camp.'" Susan Sontag, "Notes on 'Camp,'" in *Against Interpretation and Other Essays* (London: Penguin, 2009).

2. Montesquieu, *The Spirit of the Laws*, trans. and ed. Anne M. Cohler, Basia Carolyn Miller, and Harold Samuel Stone (Cambridge: Cambridge University Press, 1989), p. 310.

1. Cute as a Weapon of Mass Seduction

1. Nietzsche praises the Greeks for lingering "courageously at the surface" and so for being

"superficial—*out of profundity*." Friedrich Nietzsche, "Preface for the Second Edition," *The Gay Science*, trans. Walter Kaufmann (New York: Random House, 1974), §4, p. 38.

2. For a superb discussion of Heidegger on ungroundedness, see Katherine Withy, *Heidegger on Being Uncanny* (Cambridge, MA: Harvard University Press, 2015).

3. Sontag, "Notes on 'Camp,'" p. 275.

4. Sontag, "Notes on 'Camp,'" p. 288; cf. p. 283.

5. Gary Genosko, *Félix Guattari: An Aberrant Introduction* (London and New York: Continuum, 2002), p. 115.

6. Others have also seen *Balloon Dog* as exemplifying cuteness. See, for example, Elizabeth Legge's sophisticated account in "When Awe turns to Awww: Jeff Koons's *Balloon Dog* and the Cute Sublime," in *The Aesthetics and Affects of Cuteness*, ed. Joshua Paul Dale, Joyce Goggin, Julia Leyda, Anthony P. McIntyre, and Diane Negra (New York and London: Routledge, 2017), pp. 130–150.

7. Christine R. Yano, *Pink Globalization: Hello Kitty's Trek across the Pacific* (Durham, NC, and London: Duke University Press, 2013), p. 8.

8. I owe these facts to Laura Tangley, in Amy Crawford, "Q&A with Laura Tangley," *Smithsonian Magazine*, May 31, 2006; and to Natalie Angier, "The Cute Factor," *New York Times*, January 3, 2006. The penguin documentary in question is the 2005 *March of the Penguins*.

9. Sianne Ngai, *Our Aesthetic Categories: Zany, Cute, Interesting* (Cambridge, MA, and London: Harvard University Press, 2012), pp. 3, 24, 64, and 85.

10. Yano, *Pink Globalization*, p. 22.

11. Yano, *Pink Globalization*, p. 167, citing Annalee Newitz, "The Apotheosis of Cute," *San Francisco Bay Guardian*, June 3, 2002.

12. Gary S. Cross, *The Cute and the Cool: Wondrous Innocence and Modern American Children's Culture* (New York: Oxford University Press, 2004), pp. 4 and 43.

13. Angier articulates Dutton's position in Angier, "The Cute Factor."

14. Sharon Kinsella, "Comments on McVeigh (1996)," *Journal of Material Culture* 2 (3), 1997, pp. 383–387; see p. 383.

15. Daniel Harris, *Cute, Quaint, Hungry, and Romantic: The Aesthetics of Consumerism* (New

York: Basic Books, 2000), pp. 21, 15, 13, and 5.

16. Daniel Harris, *Cute, Quaint, Hungry, and Romantic*, pp. 12, 11, 12, 7, and *passim*.

17. Joshua Paul Dale, "The Appeal of the Cute Object," in Dale et al., *The Aesthetics and Affects of Cuteness*, pp. 35–55; see p. 52.

18. Gary D. Sherman and Jonathan Haidt, "Cuteness and Disgust: The Humanizing and Dehumanizing Effects of Emotion," in *Emotion Review* 3 (3), July 2011, pp. 245–251. Quotes are from pp. 248 and 250.

2. Spooked in the Garden of Eden

1. Konrad Lorenz, *Studies in Animal and Human Behaviour,* vol. 2, trans. Robert Martin (London: Methuen, 1971), pp. 154–156; cf. Konrad Lorenz, *The Foundations of Ethology*, trans. Konrad Z. Lorenz and Robert Warren Kickert (New York and Vienna: Springer Verlag, 1981), pp. 162–165.

2. Gary Cross, *The Cute and the Cool*, p. 5.

3. I owe this summary of the traits of E.T. to Gary Genosko, *Félix Guattari*, p. 115.

4. I owe the examples of Winnie the Pooh, Disney's 101 Dalmatians, Little Mutt, and So Shy Sherri, as well as the phrase "anatomical disaster," to Daniel Harris, *Cute, Quaint, Hungry, and Romantic*, pp. 1–6 and 3.

5. Sigmund Freud, "The 'Uncanny' (1919)" in *The Standard Edition of the Complete Psychological Works of Sigmund Freud*, ed. and trans. James Strachey (London: Hogarth, 1955), vol. 17, pp. 217–256. Several authors have already noted the connection between Cute and the uncanny, as discussed by Freud. For example, see Joel Gn, "On the Curious Case of Machine Cuteness," in Dale et al., *The Aesthetics and Affects of Cuteness*, pp. 175–193.

6. Lorenz, *The Foundations of Ethology*, pp. 164–165.

3. Cute as an Uncertainty Principle

1. I owe this summary and interpretation of the myth to Luc Brisson, *Sexual Ambivalence*, trans. Janet Lloyd (Berkeley and London: University of California Press, 2002),

pp. 42–60. Brisson cites Ovid, *Metamorphoses* IV, 285–388, on p. 48.

2. Una Roman D'Elia, "Grotesque Painting and Painting as Grotesque in the Renaissance," *Notes in the History of Art* 33 (2), 2014, pp. 5–12, see p. 5. D'Elia cites Vasari, and adds: "This passage is in both the 1550 edition (Book I: 'Proemio,' ch. XXVII) and the 1568 edition (Book I: 'Introduzione della pittura,' ch. XIII). . . . Giorgio Vasari, *Le Opere*, ed. Gaetano Milanesi, 9 vols. (Florence: Sansoni, 1906), I, p. 193."

3. Sontag, "Notes on 'Camp,'" p. 280.

4. See Clement Greenberg, "Avant-Garde and Kitsch," in *Art and Culture* (Boston: Beacon, 1961), p. 9 *passim*.

5. This quotation is taken from a comment on "Prize and No Prize, or What's a Baby? Infantine and Maternal Jealousy," in the *New York Picayune*, found in "The Baby Show Exhibit," Lost Museum Archive, City University of New York, http://lostmuseum.cuny.edu /archive/exhibit/baby/. This archive includes further information about Barnum's American Museum and baby shows. For another

newspaper report from that time see "The Baby Show," *New York Times*, June 6, 1855. My discussion of baby shows and these references are indebted to Angela Sorby, "'A Dimple in the Tomb': Cuteness in Emily Dickinson," *ESQ: A Journal of Nineteenth-Century American Literature and Culture*, 63 (2), 2017, pp. 297–328; see p. 311. My remarks on Tom Thumb and Phineas Taylor Barnum are also indebted to the excellent article on the website of London's Victoria & Albert Museum, http://www.vam.ac.uk/content/articles/t/tom-thumb/.

6. "The Loving Lilliputians," *New York Times*, February 11, 1863.
7. Ngai, *Our Aesthetic Categories*, p. 15.
8. Ngai, *Our Aesthetic Categories*, pp. 12–13.
9. Ngai, *Our Aesthetic Categories*, pp. 76–77.
10. Cross, *The Cute and the Cool*, p. 43.
11. "Cute," Merriam-Webster.com.
12. Cross, *The Cute and the Cool*, pp. 57–58 and 65. My remarks on Shirley Temple are indebted to Cross.
13. G.W.F. Hegel, "Independence and Dependence of Self-Consciousness: Lordship and Bondage," in *Phenomenology of Spirit*, trans.

A. V. Miller (Oxford: Oxford University Press, 1979), pp. 111–119.

14. Harris, *Cute, Quaint, Hungry, and Romantic*, p. 6.

15. Friedrich Nietzsche, *Beyond Good and Evil*, in *Basic Writings of Nietzsche*, trans. Walter Kaufmann (New York: Modern Library, 1968), pp. 181–435, §§13, 186, 211, and 289 (my italics).

16. Anthony Giddens, *The Transformation of Intimacy: Sexuality, Love and Eroticism in Modern Societies* (Cambridge: Polity Press, 1992), p. 171. I am indebted to Giddens's remarks on Foucault's account of sexuality and power relations: pp. 18–19 and 169–171.

4. Mickey Mouse and the Cuteness Continuum

1. Konrad Lorenz, "Die angeborenen Formen möglicher Erfahrung," *Zeitschrift Tierpsychologie* 5, 1943, pp. 235–409; and Lorenz, *Studies in Animal and Human Behaviour*, vol. 2, p. 154. I owe the summary of Lorenz's features of infants to John Morreall, "Cuteness,"

British Journal of Aesthetics 31 (1), January 1991, pp. 39-47.

2. Stephen Jay Gould, "A Biological Homage to Mickey Mouse," in *The Panda's Thumb: More Reflections in Natural History* (New York and London: W. W. Norton, 1982), pp. 95-107; see p. 95.

3. Gould, "A Biological Homage to Mickey Mouse," p. 95.

4. Picture and text quoted, with adaptations, from Gould, "A Biological Homage to Mickey Mouse," pp. 96-97. Picture copyright: Walt Disney Productions.

5. Gary Genosko, "Natures and Cultures of Cuteness," in *InVisible Culture: An Electronic Journal for Visual Culture.* Issue 9, Fall 2005. Visual & Cultural Studies Program, University of Rochester, p. 1.

6. I owe this suggestion to Christopher Finch, who argues that "Mickey . . . had become virtually a national symbol, and as such he was expected to behave properly at all times. If he occasionally stepped out of line, any number of letters would arrive at the Studio from citizens and organizations who felt that the nation's moral well-being was in their hands. . . .

Eventually he would be pressured into the role of straight man." Quoted in Gould, "A Biological Homage to Mickey Mouse," p. 96.

7. Gould, "A Biological Homage to Mickey Mouse," p. 97.

8. See, for example, Lorenz, *Studies in Animal and Human Behaviour*, pp. 154-156; cf. Lorenz, *The Foundations of Ethology*, pp. 153-162.

5. *Kawaii*: The New Japanese Imperium

1. Martin Heidegger, *Being and Time*, trans. John Macquarrie and Edward Robinson (Oxford: Blackwell, 1962), pp. 174-176 and 230-235.

2. Yano, *Pink Globalization*, p. 46.

3. Sharon Kinsella, "Cuties in Japan," in *Women, Media and Consumption in Japan*, ed. Lise Skov and Brian Moeran (Honolulu: University of Hawaii Press, 1995), pp. 220-254; see p. 244. Kinsella expands fascinatingly on this "intense male cultural interest in and production of" girl characters in modern Japan in "Minstrelized Girls: Male Performers of Japan's Lolita Complex," *Japan Forum* 18 (1), March 2006, pp. 65-87; see p. 65.

4. Cited by Kinsella, "Cuties in Japan," pp. 220-221. Originally published in *CREA Magazine* (Japan), November 1992, p. 58.

5. Kinsella, "Cuties in Japan," p. 237.

6. Takashi Murakami, "Earth in My Window," in *Little Boy: The Arts of Japan's Exploding Subculture*, ed. Takashi Murakami (New Haven, CT: Yale University Press; New York: Japan Society, 2005), pp. 100-101.

7. From Christine R. Yano, "Wink on Pink: Interpreting Japanese Cute as It Grabs the Global Headlines," *Journal of Asian Studies* 68 (3), 2009, p. 685.

8. Matt Alt, "Japan's Cute Army," *New Yorker*, November 30, 2015. This paragraph and the next are indebted to Alt's article.

9. Alt, "Japan's Cute Army."

10. Marilyn Ivy, "The Art of Cute Little Things: Nara Yoshitomo's Parapolitics," *Mechademia* 5, 2010, pp. 3-29; see p. 5.

11. I first noticed this image in Ivy, "The Art of Cute Little Things," p. 8, to which I am indebted.

12. Quote and citation from Roger Scruton, *The Aesthetics of Music* (Oxford: Oxford University

Press, 1999), p. 464. The translation is to be found in Donald Keene, *World Within Walls: Japanese Literature of the Pre-Modern Era 1600–1867* (New York: Columbia University Press, 1999).

13. Matsuo Basho, *Basho: The Complete Haiku*, trans. Jane Reichhold (Tokyo, New York, and London: Kodansha International, 2008), pp. 165 and 342.

14. This sentence is indebted to Anne Allison, "Cuteness as Japan's Millennial Product," in *Pikachu's Global Adventure: The Rise and Fall of Pokémon*, ed. Joseph Tobin (Durham, NC, and London: Duke University Press, 2004), pp. 34–49 and 34–35.

15. Dani Cavallaro, *Art in Anime: The Creative Quest as Theme and Metaphor* (Jefferson, NC, and London: McFarland, 2012), p. 46.

16. Sei Shōnagon, *The Pillow Book of Sei Shōnagon*, vol. 1, trans. Ivan Morris (New York: Columbia University Press, 1967), pp. 156–157. I thank Joshua Dale for referring me to *The Pillow Book*.

17. Miura Jun, *An Illustrated Guide to Yuru Chara* (Tokyo: Fusosha, 2004), cited in Murakami,

ed., *Little Boy: The Arts of Japan's Exploding Subculture*, p. 86.

18. I thank Jessica Frazier for these references to the storm god and to *Princess Mononoke* as exemplars of Japanese Cute. For the story of Amaterasu and Susa-no-o, see, for example, *The Kojiki: An Account of Ancient Matters*, ed. Ō No Yasumaro, trans. Gustav Heldt, pp. 23–24.

19. Katy Siegel, "In the Air," in Murakami, ed., *Little Boy: The Arts of Japan's Exploding Subculture*, p. 283.

20. Brian McVeigh, "Commodifying Affection, Authority and Gender in the Everyday Objects of Japan," *Journal of Material Culture* 1 (3), November 1996, pp. 291–312; see p. 302. Sharon Kinsella explains that "Young people dressing themselves up as innocent babes in the woods in cute styles were known as *burikko* (fake-children), a term coined by teen starlet Yamada Kuniko in 1980. The noun spawned a verb *burikko suru* (to fake-child-it), or more simply *buri buri suru* (to fake-it)." Kinsella, "Cuties in Japan," p. 225.

21. Cited in Olivia Waxman, "Hello Kitty at 40: Sexist Throwback or Empowering Icon?" *Time*, October 31, 2014.

22. McVeigh, "Commodifying Affection, Authority and Gender in the Everyday Objects of Japan," p. 308.

23. Sherman and Haidt, "Cuteness and Disgust: The Humanizing and Dehumanizing Effects of Emotion," p. 248.

6. The Cuteness of Kim Jong-il

1. Kinsella, "Minstrelized Girls," pp. 76-77.

2. B. R. Myers, *The Cleanest Race: How North Koreans See Themselves—And Why It Matters* (New York: Melville House, 2010), pp. 109-110.

3. Myers, *The Cleanest Race*, p. 101.

4. These examples are drawn from Eva Wiseman, "Addicted to Cute," *Guardian*, June 12, 2011.

7. Cute and the Uncanny

1. Freud, "The 'Uncanny,'" p. 241. Or, as he also puts it: "[T]he *unheimlich* is what was once *heimlich*, familiar; the prefix '*un*' is the token

of repression" (p. 245). My allusions to Freud and the uncanny are indebted to Katherine Withy's excellent discussion in Withy, *Heidegger on Being Uncanny*, pp. 22–28.

2. Freud, "The 'Uncanny,'" p. 220.
3. Ngai, *Our Aesthetic Categories*, p. 3.

8. What's Wrong with Cute Anthropomorphism?

1. Harris, *Cute, Quaint, Hungry, and Romantic*, pp. 4 and 11–13 *passim*.
2. Ngai, *Our Aesthetic Categories*, p. 91.
3. Francis Ponge, *L'Orange*, 1942, from *The Voice of Things*, trans. Beth Archer (New York: McGraw-Hill, 1972), p. 36. Cited in Ngai, *Our Aesthetic Categories*, pp. 90–91.
4. Ngai, *Our Aesthetic Categories*, p. 91.
5. Ngai, *Our Aesthetic Categories*, p. 85.
6. Ngai, *Our Aesthetic Categories*, p. 92.
7. Ngai, *Our Aesthetic Categories*, pp. 108, 98, and 93.
8. Sorby, "'A Dimple in the Tomb,'" p. 299.
9. I owe the example of this poem to Sorby, "'A Dimple in the Tomb,'" p. 320. Sorby cites

Dickinson, "Letter 641," *Letters of Emily Dickinson,* ed. Thomas H. Johnson and Theodora Ward (Cambridge, MA: Harvard University Press, 1958), 3: 661.

10. Homer, *The Odyssey*, trans. Robert Fagles (New York: Viking Penguin, 2006), 10.619–622, p. 248.

11. From Emily Dickinson, *The Complete Poems of Emily Dickinson,* ed. Thomas H. Johnson (Toronto: Little, Brown, 1961), 61, p. 32.

12. I thank Jeremiah Unterman for these biblical references.

13. Genesis 6:19.

14. Proverbs 6:6–8; cf. Proverbs 30:24–28.

15. Ecclesiastes 3:19–21.

16. Sherman and Haidt, "Cuteness and Disgust," pp. 245–248 *passim.*

17. This kind of either/or is not unique to the cuteness response. It is also true for compassion, which literally means "feeling with" or "suffering with," as in the German word *Mitleid.* Like Cute, compassion has a history of controversy, but one that is far more ancient and sophisticated. One tradition, descending from Aristotle, two and a half millennia ago, and

proceeding through Rousseau and Schopenhauer in the eighteenth and nineteenth centuries, argues in favor of it while another, from the Greek and Roman Stoics through Spinoza, Kant, and Nietzsche, warns of its dangers. Martha Nussbaum elegantly summarizes and evaluates these warring traditions in *Upheavals of Thought: The Intelligence of Emotions* (New York: Cambridge University Press, 2001), especially pp. 301–342 and 356–392.

18. Ngai, *Our Aesthetic Categories*, pp. 64 and 3.

9. Cute and the Monstrous: The Case of Donald Trump

1. I thank Robert Jackson for encouraging me to explore the connection between the cute and the monstrous. Maja Brzozowska-Brywczyńska has also discussed the relation of the monstrous to cuteness in an interesting essay: "Monstrous/Cute: Notes on the Ambivalent Nature of Cuteness," in Niall Scott, ed., *Monsters and the Monstrous: Myths and Metaphors of Enduring Evil* (Amsterdam: Editions Rodopi, 2007).

2. I owe these examples of the monstrous to "Monstrous and Imaginary Subjects," in *Encyclopedia of World Art*, vol. 10, ed. Bernard S. Myers (London: McGraw-Hill, 1965), cols. 250–272; see cols. 251–254.

3. *Encyclopedia of World Art*, vol. 10, cols. 252–253; see col. 252.

4. I owe this characterization of the grotesque to Wolfgang Kayser, who, in a classic study of the subject, sees it as "an attempt to invoke and subdue the demonic aspects of the world." Wolfgang Kayser, *The Grotesque in Art and Literature*, trans. Ulrich Weisstein (New York: Columbia University Press, 1981), p. 188. Thomas Cramer, in his own book on the topic, offers a slightly different definition of the grotesque that is also relevant to an understanding of Donald Trump, namely as "the defeat, by means of the comic, of anxiety in the face of the inexplicable." Thomas Cramer, *Das Groteske bei E. T. A. Hoffmann* (Munich, 1966), p. 26, cited and translated in Michael Steig, "Defining the Grotesque: An Attempt at Synthesis," *Journal of Aesthetics and Art Criticism* 29 (2), Winter 1970, pp. 253–260; see p. 256; see also n. 9.

5. In Steig, "Defining the Grotesque," p. 255.
6. Thierry Goater, "An 'Uncanny Revel': The Poetics and Politics of the Grotesque in Thomas Hardy's *The Mayor of Casterbridge*," in *The Grotesque in the Fiction of Charles Dickens and Other 19th-Century European Novelists*, ed. Isabelle Hervouet-Farrar and Max Vega-Ritter (Newcastle upon Tyne: Cambridge Scholars Publishing, 2014), pp. 133–149; see p. 147.

10. Cute and the New Cult of the Child

1. As I argue in *Love: A New Understanding of an Ancient Emotion*, the elevation of childhood to sacred status is of a piece with the striking way in which the child is gradually replacing the romantic partner as the archetypal object of love, and has been ever since the end of the nineteenth century—just as before that, from the late eighteenth century, the romantic partner began to displace God as the supreme object of love. Contrary to what we might expect, this elevation of the child is not, I suggest there, the result of craving a lost innocence or otherwise of

fetishizing innocence; nor is it a new way of seeking immortality in a world that no longer believes in an afterlife; nor, too, is it explained by declining child mortality, which has made it "safer" to invest love and value in one's children. Instead, it is "the result of a concatenation of typically modern impulses that have slowly taken powerful root since the late eighteenth century." The most important such impulses, I propose, are these: "the desire to locate the sacred in the everyday world, instead of in transcendence of it, such as in God or in a romantic union that is taken to abolish the distinct individuality of the lovers; the war on risk and suffering that marks our age, a war to which the security of the child has become totemic; the unprecedented degree to which childhood has come to be seen as *the* key to a flourishing life; the value placed on individual autonomy, to which love for the child is . . . far more attuned than is, say, romantic love; and a turn away from the belief that love can have a final goal, such as union with the loved one, or be marked by an event that 'consummates' it, in the sense that it could have in traditional conceptions of love for God or the romantic partner." See Simon May, *Love: A New Understanding of an Ancient Emotion* (New York: Oxford University Press, 2019), p. xviii; cf. chapter 33 *passim*.

2. Neil Postman, *The Disappearance of Childhood* (New York: Delacorte, 1982).

3. Sharon Stephens, "Children and the Politics of Culture in 'Late Capitalism,'" in *Children and the Politics of Culture*, ed. Sharon Stephens (Princeton, NJ: Princeton University Press, 1995), p. 9, cited in Allison James, Chris Jenks, and Alan Prout, *Theorizing Childhood* (Oxford: Polity, 1998), p. 85.

4. Philippe Ariès, *Centuries of Childhood: A Social History of Family Life*, trans. Robert Baldick (London: Random House, 1996), particularly pp. 31–47.

5. Vernon Reynolds describes empirical research supporting the idea of childhood as "a completely different world, so different that we seem to be confronted by a different order of being." Vernon Reynolds, "Can There Be an Anthropology of Children? A Reply," *Journal*

    of the Anthropological Society of Oxford 5 (1), 1974, pp. 32–38, see p. 34; cited in James, Jenks, and Prout, *Theorizing Childhood*, p. 85.

6. Viviana A. Zelizer, *Pricing the Priceless Child* (Princeton, NJ: Princeton University Press, 1994), p. 5.

7. Walter I. Trattner, *Crusade for the Children: A History of the National Child Labor Committee and Child Labor Reform in America* (Chicago: Quadrangle, 1970), pp. 11–12, quoted in Hugh D. Hindman, *Child Labor: An American History* (New York: M. E. Sharpe, 2002), p. 51.

8. Zelizer, *Pricing the Priceless Child*, p. 6.

9. Zelizer, *Pricing the Priceless Child*, p. 3.

10. Zelizer, *Pricing the Priceless Child*, pp. 5–6.

11. Zelizer, *Pricing the Priceless Child*, p. 6.

12. Zelizer, *Pricing the Priceless Child*, p. 14. Gary Cross writes that the demand for infants rose from only 19–21 percent of American adoptions in the 1930s to 48 percent in 1950 and 68 percent in 1960, and that by the end of the 1970s it had reached 98 percent. Cross, *The Cute and the Cool*, p. 30.

13. Zelizer, *Pricing the Priceless Child*, p. 23.

14. Zelizer, *Pricing the Priceless Child*, p. 29.

15. Ruth S. Kempe and C. Henry Kempe, *Child Abuse* (London: Fontana, 1978), p. 15.
16. William Wordsworth, "Ode: Intimations of Immortality from Recollections of Early Childhood."

11. Survival of the Cutest

1. Ngai, *Our Aesthetic Categories*, p. 54.
2. Quotations in this paragraph are from Yano, *Pink Globalization*, p. 160 (my italics).
3. Neil Steinberg, "The New Science of Cute," *Guardian*, July 19, 2016.

12. Cute and Kitsch: Identical Twins?

1. Tomas Kulka, *Kitsch and Art* (University Park: Pennsylvania State University Press, 1996), p. 16.
2. Hermann Broch, "Notes on the Problem of Kitsch," in *Kitsch: The World of Bad Taste*, ed. Gillo Dorfles (New York: Universe Books, 1969), pp. 49–76; see p. 76.
3. Broch, "Notes on the Problem of Kitsch," p. 63.
4. Greenberg, "Avant-Garde and Kitsch," p. 10.

5. Karsten Harries, *The Meaning of Modern Art* (Evanston, IL: Northwestern University Press, 1968), p. 77. I owe this reference to Robert C. Solomon, "On Kitsch and Sentimentality," *Journal of Aesthetics and Art Criticism* 49 (1), Winter 1991, p. 4, n. 12.

6. Cited in Whitney Rugg, "Kitsch," Theories of Media Keywords Glossary, http://csmt.uchicago.edu/glossary2004/kitsch.htm.

7. I thank Andrew Huddleston for pointing out to me this distinction between Kitsch that has pretensions to be deep and cheap trinkets that have no such pretensions.

8. Solomon, "On Kitsch and Sentimentality," p. 5 *passim*.

9. Arthur C. Danto, *The Abuse of Beauty* (Chicago and La Salle, IL: Open Court, 2003), p. 21.

10. Milan Kundera, *The Unbearable Lightness of Being*, trans. Michael Henry Heim (London: Faber and Faber, 1985), p. 244.

11. Sontag, "Notes on 'Camp,'" p. 284.

12. Tomas Kulka, "Kitsch," *British Journal of Aesthetics* 28 (1), Winter 1988, pp. 18–27; see pp. 20 and 23.

13. Solomon, "On Kitsch and Sentimentality," p. 5.
14. Kundera, *The Unbearable Lightness of Being*, p. 242.

13. Exiting the Cult of Sincerity

1. Cited in Lionel Trilling, *Sincerity and Authenticity* (Cambridge, MA: Harvard University Press, 1973), p. 6.
2. Jean-Jacques Rousseau, *Confessions*, trans. P. N. Furbank (New York: Knopf, 1992), bk. 1, p. 1 (my italics).
3. David Hume to the Countess de Boufflers, January 19, 1766 (personal letter), in David Hume, *Private Correspondence of David Hume with Several Distinguished Persons, Between the Years 1761 and 1776* (London: Henry Colburn, 1820), p. 125. Cited in Bernard Williams, *Truth and Truthfulness: An Essay in Genealogy* (Princeton, NJ: Princeton University Press, 2002), p. 177.
4. This discussion is indebted to Trilling, *Sincerity and Authenticity*, especially pp. 8–11.

14. "Lifetime Is a Child at Play"

1. Friedrich Nietzsche, "The Four Great Errors," in *Twilight of the Idols*, in *The Portable Nietzsche*, ed. and trans. Walter Kaufmann (New York: Viking, 1976), §§7–8, pp. 499–501.

2. Friedrich Nietzsche, "On the Three Metamorphoses," in *Thus Spoke Zarathustra*, in *The Portable Nietzsche*, ed. and trans. Walter Kaufmann (New York: Viking, 1976), p. 139.

3. Friedrich Nietzsche, *The Will to Power*, trans. Walter Kaufmann and R. J. Hollingdale (New York: Vintage, 1968), §797, p. 419, n. 125. *Pais Paizon* is the Greek for "a child playing" and alludes to the fragment of Heraclitus that I go on to cite.

4. Nietzsche, *Beyond Good and Evil*, §94, p. 273.

5. Heraclitus, fragment XCIV (Diels Kranz 52), cited in Charles H. Kahn, *The Art and Thought of Heraclitus* (Cambridge: Cambridge University Press, 1979), pp. 70–71.

Bibliography

Allison, Anne, "Cuteness as Japan's Millennial Product," in *Pikachu's Global Adventure: The Rise and Fall of Pokémon*, ed. Joseph Tobin (Durham, NC, and London: Duke University Press, 2004), pp. 34–49.

Alt, Matt, "Japan's Cute Army," *New Yorker*, November 30, 2015.

Angier, Natalie, "The Cute Factor," *New York Times*, January 3, 2006.

Ariès, Philippe, *Centuries of Childhood: A Social History of Family Life*, trans. Robert Baldick (London: Random House, 1996).

Basho, Matsuo, *Basho: The Complete Haiku*, trans. Jane Reichhold (Tokyo, New York, and London: Kodansha International, 2008).

Brisson, Luc, *Sexual Ambivalence*, trans. Janet Lloyd (Berkeley and London: University of California Press, 2002).

Broch, Hermann, "Notes on the Problem of Kitsch," in *Kitsch: The World of Bad Taste*, ed. Gillo Dorfles (New York: Universe Books, 1969), pp. 49–76.

Brzozowska-Brywczyńska, Maja, "Monstrous/Cute: Notes on the Ambivalent Nature of Cuteness," in *Monsters and the Monstrous: Myths and Metaphors of Enduring Evil*, ed. Niall Scott (Amsterdam: Editions Rodopi, 2007).

Cavallaro, Dani, *Art in Anime: The Creative Quest as Theme and Metaphor* (Jefferson, NC, and London: McFarland, 2012).

Crawford, Amy, "Q&A with Laura Tangley," *Smithsonian Magazine*, May 31, 2006.

Cross, Gary S., *The Cute and the Cool: Wondrous Innocence and Modern American Children's Culture* (New York: Oxford University Press, 2004).

Dale, Joshua Paul, Joyce Goggin, Julia Leyda, Anthony P. McIntyre, and Diane Negra, eds., *The Aesthetics and Affects of Cuteness* (New York and London: Routledge, 2017).

Danto, Arthur C., *The Abuse of Beauty* (Chicago and La Salle, IL: Open Court, 2003).

D'Elia, Una Roman, "Grotesque Painting and Painting as Grotesque in the Renaissance,"

Notes in the History of Art 33 (2), 2014, pp. 5–12.

Dickinson, Emily, *The Complete Poems of Emily Dickinson*, ed. Thomas H. Johnson (Toronto: Little, Brown, 1961).

Encyclopedia of World Art, vol. 10, ed. Bernard S. Myers (London: McGraw-Hill, 1965).

Freud, Sigmund, "The 'Uncanny' (1919)," in *The Standard Edition of the Complete Psychological Works of Sigmund Freud*, ed. and trans. James Strachey (London: Hogarth, 1955), vol. 17, pp. 217–256.

Genosko, Gary, *Félix Guattari: An Aberrant Introduction* (London and New York: Continuum, 2002).

——, "Natures and Cultures of Cuteness," *In-Visible Culture: An Electronic Journal for Visual Culture.* Issue 9, Fall 2005. Visual & Cultural Studies Program, University of Rochester.

Giddens, Anthony, *The Transformation of Intimacy: Sexuality, Love and Eroticism in Modern Societies* (Cambridge: Polity Press, 1992).

Gn, Joel, "On the Curious Case of Machine Cuteness," in *The Aesthetics and Affects of Cuteness*, ed. Joshua Paul Dale, Joyce Goggin, Julia Leyda, Anthony P. McIntyre, and Diane Negra (New York and London: Routledge, 2017).

Goater, Thierry, "An 'Uncanny Revel': The Poetics and Politics of the Grotesque in Thomas Hardy's *The Mayor of Casterbridge*," in *The Grotesque in the Fiction of Charles Dickens and Other 19th-Century European Novelists*, ed. Isabelle Hervouet-Farrar and Max Vega-Ritter (Newcastle upon Tyne: Cambridge Scholars Publishing, 2014), pp. 133-149.

Gould, Stephen Jay, "A Biological Homage to Mickey Mouse," in *The Panda's Thumb: More Reflections in Natural History* (New York and London: W. W. Norton, 1982), pp. 95-107.

Greenberg, Clement, *Art and Culture* (Boston: Beacon, 1961).

Harries, Karsten, *The Meaning of Modern Art* (Evanston, IL: Northwestern University Press, 1968).

Harris, Daniel, *Cute, Quaint, Hungry, and Romantic: The Aesthetics of Consumerism* (New York: Basic Books, 2000).

Hegel, G.W.F., *Phenomenology of Spirit*, trans. A. V. Miller (Oxford: Oxford University Press, 1979).

Heidegger, Martin, *Being and Time*, trans. John Macquarrie and Edward Robinson (Oxford: Blackwell, 1962).

Hindman, Hugh D., *Child Labor: An American History* (New York: M. E. Sharpe, 2002).

Homer, *The Odyssey*, trans. Robert Fagles (New York: Viking Penguin, 2006).

Hume, David, *Private Correspondence of David Hume with Several Distinguished Persons, Between the Years 1761 and 1776* (London: Henry Colburn, 1820).

Ivy, Marilyn, "The Art of Cute Little Things: Nara Yoshitomo's Parapolitics," *Mechademia* 5, (2010), pp. 3–29.

James, Allison, Chris Jenks, and Alan Prout, *Theorizing Childhood* (Oxford: Polity Press, 1998).

Kahn, Charles H., *The Art and Thought of Heraclitus* (Cambridge: Cambridge University Press, 1979).

Kayser, Wolfgang, *The Grotesque in Art and Literature*, trans. Ulrich Weisstein (New York: Columbia University Press, 1981).

Kempe, Ruth S., and C. Henry Kempe, *Child Abuse* (London: Fontana, 1978).

Kinsella, Sharon, "Comments on McVeigh (1996)," *Journal of Material Culture* 2 (3), 1997, pp. 383–387.

——, "Cuties in Japan," in *Women, Media and Consumption in Japan*, ed. Lise Skov and Brian Moeran (Honolulu: University of Hawaii Press, 1995), pp. 220–254.

——, "Minstrelized Girls: Male Performers of Japan's Lolita Complex," in *Japan Forum* 18 (1), March 2006, pp. 65–87.

Kulka, Tomas, "Kitsch," *British Journal of Aesthetics* 28 (1), Winter 1988, pp. 18–27.

——, *Kitsch and Art* (University Park: Pennsylvania State University Press, 1996).

Kundera, Milan, *The Unbearable Lightness of Being*, trans. Michael Henry Heim (London: Faber and Faber, 1985).

Legge, Elizabeth, "When Awe Turns to Awww: Jeff Koons's *Balloon Dog* and the Cute Sublime," in *The Aesthetics and Affects of Cuteness*, ed. Joshua Paul Dale, Joyce Goggin, Julia Leyda, Anthony P. McIntyre, and Diane Negra (New York and London: Routledge, 2017).

Lorenz, Konrad, "Die angeborenen Formen möglicher Erfahrung," *Zeitschrift Tierpsychologie* 5, 1943, pp. 235–409.

——, *The Foundations of Ethology*, trans. Konrad Z. Lorenz and Robert Warren Kickert (New York and Vienna: Springer Verlag, 1981).

——, *Studies in Animal and Human Behaviour*, vol. 2, trans. Robert Martin (London: Methuen, 1971).

May, Simon, *Love: A New Understanding of an Ancient Emotion* (New York: Oxford University Press, 2019).

McVeigh, Brian, "Commodifying Affection, Authority and Gender in the Everyday Objects of Japan," *Journal of Material Culture* 1 (3), November 1996, pp. 291-312.

Miura, Jun, *An Illustrated Guide to Yuru Chara* (Tokyo: Fusosha, 2004).

Montesquieu, *The Spirit of the Laws*, trans. and ed. Anne M. Cohler, Basia Carolyn Miller, and Harold Samuel Stone (Cambridge: Cambridge University Press, 1989).

Morreall, John, "Cuteness," *British Journal of Aesthetics* 31 (1), January 1991, pp. 39-47.

Murakami, Takashi, ed., *Little Boy: The Arts of Japan's Exploding Subculture* (New Haven, CT: Yale University Press; New York: Japan Society, 2005).

Myers, B. R., *The Cleanest Race: How North Koreans See Themselves—And Why It Matters* (New York: Melville House, 2010).

Ngai, Sianne, *Our Aesthetic Categories: Zany, Cute, Interesting* (Cambridge, MA, and London: Harvard University Press, 2012).

Nietzsche, Friedrich, *Beyond Good and Evil*, in *Basic Writings of Nietzsche,* trans. Walter Kaufmann (New York: Modern Library, 1968).

——, *The Gay Science*, trans. Walter Kaufmann (New York: Random House, 1974).

——, *Thus Spoke Zarathustra*, in *The Portable Nietzsche*, ed. and trans. Walter Kaufmann (New York: Viking, 1976).

——, *Twilight of the Idols*, in *The Portable Nietzsche*, ed. and trans. Walter Kaufmann (New York: Viking, 1976).

——, *The Will to Power*, trans. Walter Kaufmann and R. J. Hollingdale (New York: Vintage, 1968).

Nussbaum, Martha, *Upheavals of Thought: The Intelligence of Emotions* (New York: Cambridge University Press, 2001).

Postman, Neil, *The Disappearance of Childhood* (New York: Delacorte, 1982).

Rousseau, Jean-Jacques, *Confessions*, trans. P. N. Furbank (New York: Knopf, 1992).

Rugg, Whitney, "Kitsch," Theories of Media Keywords Glossary, http://csmt.uchicago.edu /glossary2004/kitsch.htm.

Scruton, Roger, *The Aesthetics of Music* (Oxford: Oxford University Press, 1999).

Sherman, Gary D., and Jonathan Haidt, "Cuteness and Disgust: The Humanizing and Dehumanizing Effects of Emotion," in *Emotion Review* 3 (3), July 2011, pp. 245–251.

Shōnagon, Sei, *The Pillow Book of Sei Shōnagon*, vol. 1, trans. Ivan Morris (New York: Columbia University Press, 1967).

Solomon, Robert C., "On Kitsch and Sentimentality," *Journal of Aesthetics and Art Criticism* 49 (1), Winter 1991, pp. 1–14.

Sontag, Susan, "Notes on 'Camp'," in *Against Interpretation and Other Essays* (London: Penguin, 2009), pp. 275–292.

Sorby, Angela, "'A Dimple in the Tomb': Cuteness in Emily Dickinson," *ESQ: A Journal of Nineteenth-Century American Literature and Culture* 63 (2), 2017, pp. 297–328.

Steig, Michael, "Defining the Grotesque: An Attempt at Synthesis," *Journal of Aesthetics and Art Criticism* 29 (2), Winter 1970, pp. 253–260.

Steinberg, Neil, "The New Science of Cute," *Guardian*, July 19, 2016.

Trattner, Walter I., *Crusade for the Children: A History of the National Child Labor Committee and Child Labor Reform in America* (Chicago: Quadrangle, 1970).

Trilling, Lionel, *Sincerity and Authenticity* (Cambridge, MA: Harvard University Press, 1973).

Waxman, Olivia, "Hello Kitty at 40: Sexist Throwback or Empowering Icon?" *Time*, October 31, 2014.

Williams, Bernard, *Truth and Truthfulness: An Essay in Genealogy* (Princeton, NJ: Princeton University Press, 2002).

Wiseman, Eva, "Addicted to Cute," *Guardian*, 12 June, 2011.

Withy, Katherine, *Heidegger on Being Uncanny* (Cambridge, MA: Harvard University Press, 2015).

Yano, Christine R., *Pink Globalization: Hello Kitty's Trek across the Pacific* (Durham, NC, and London: Duke University Press, 2013).

———, "Wink on Pink: Interpreting Japanese Cute as It Grabs the Global Headlines," *Journal of Asian Studies* 68 (3), August 2009, pp. 681–688.

Yasumaro, Ō No, ed., *The Kojiki: An Account of Ancient Matters*, trans. Gustav Heldt (New York: Columbia University Press, 2014).

Zelizer, Viviana A., *Pricing the Priceless Child: The Changing Social Value of Children* (Princeton, NJ: Princeton University Press, 1994).

Index